THE PONY CI BOOK
Number 2

First published in Great Britain
by Threshold Books Limited,
661 Fulham Road, London SW6 5PZ

© Threshold Books Limited 1988

British Library Cataloguing in
Publication Data

The Pony Club book number two.
1. Livestock: Ponies – For children
I. Pony Club
636.1'6

ISBN 0-901366-17-X

Designed by Eddie Poulton

Printed and bound in Spain by
Graficas Estella S.A., Navarre.

CONTENTS

Views from Bridle Paths

Carole Vincer

1. In Town

Wildlife in urban areas depends greatly on the surrounding countryside and the regional variations of life which it contains. Some species cannot penetrate further than the city suburbs. Others have adapted, and thrive in abundance.

Here are some of the most common and striking examples that you are likely to see: Resident birds and summer visitors. Birds on or near water. Simple plant life on walls. Buddleia, the 'butterfly bush'. Trees: easily identified by their leaves, or twigs in winter. Colourful fungi. The active rodent.

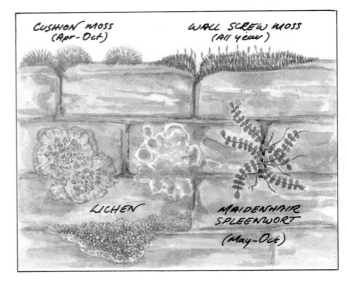

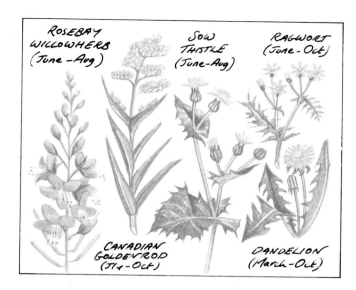

ROSEBAY
WILLOWHERB
(June - Aug)

SOW
THISTLE
(June - Aug)

RAGWORT
(June - Oct)

CANADIAN
GOLDENROD
(Jly - Oct)

DANDELION
(March - Oct)

RED ADMIRAL
(May - Oct)

SMALL WHITE
(April - Sep)

PEACOCK
(March - Oct)

SMALL TORTOISESHELL
(All year)

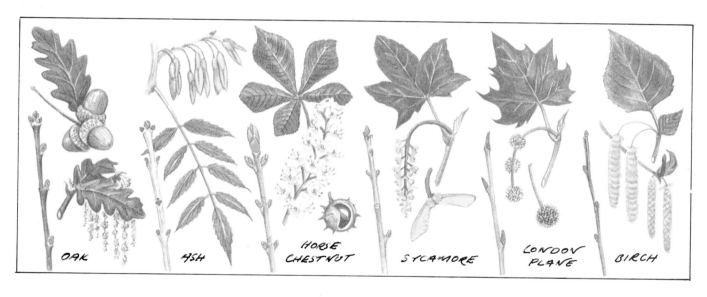

OAK

ASH

HORSE
CHESTNUT

SYCAMORE

LONDON
PLANE

BIRCH

SULPHUR TUFT
(Aug - Nov)

BEEFSTEAK
(Aug - Nov)

BRACKET FUNGI (All year)

GREY SQUIRREL

Word Search with Clues

Answer the clues and find the single word in the word search.
There are no surplus letters but many are used more than once.

Answers are on page 63.

20 ___ tail

10 An ounce of blood is worth a ___ of bone

17 ___ No. 13

16 A bad ___

9 Opposite to thin ___

8 Golden horse _ _ _ _ _ _ _ _

7 _ _ _ _

6 _ _ _ _ _ _

11 Between walk and canter _ _ _ _

14 The hound _ _ _ _ the fox

15 Tie, stock or toes: _ _ _

W	E	L	U	N	G	E	M
H	O	R	N	H	R	T	A
I	U	T	G	O	R	F	H
P	I	N	A	O	A	I	L
T	O	N	T	F	T	T	E
T	I	E	E	S	O	E	P
O	N	I	M	O	L	A	P

3 _ _ _ _

1 _ _ _ _ _

19 One of many in feed or porridge ___

12 Red, blue or chestnut _ _ _ _

21 _ _ _ _

22 _ _ _ _

5 ___ stripe

4 To _ _ _ _ _

13 EMOP : Anag.

2 _ _ _ _

18 ITE : Anag.

6

The Worldwide Pony Club

Cynthia Muir

The Pony Club is the largest association of riders in the world – and the largest youth club, too. In official terms it is 'an international voluntary organisation for those interested in ponies and riding.' Those who belong to it receive advice, instruction and encouragement, and a comradeship which is literally worldwide.

The Pony Club has come a long way since 1930, the year after its inauguration, when – at the first meeting of its Central Committee – a membership of 700 was recorded. A year later, the membership had reached 4442. During the same year – 1932 – the first Pony Club camp was held: that supreme combination of instruction, competition, hard work and fun.

Today the total membership is over 100,000, with branches in 25 countries, ranging, alphabetically, from Australia to Zimbabwe. The United Kingdom has 367 branches; overseas there are 1743. Australia, with 915 branches and 46,750 members, is the most strongly represented. The first Overseas Branch was the Royal Calpe Hunt Pony Club (Gibraltar), affiliated in 1930, but sadly this ceased to exist several years ago. The newest, formed in 1987, is Papua, New Guinea – which is run by a former West Kent Pony Club member. Most overseas branches have been in existence for twenty years or more.

Originally, branches took the name of their local hunt; and though the third largest in Britain today, the North Warwickshire, is flourishing, unfortunately the hunt of that name had to be disbanded a few seasons ago, due to the encroaching motorways and urbanisation.

The British Isles are remarkably fortunate in having so many indigenous breeds of pony. Connemara, Dales, Dartmoor, Exmoors, Fell, Highland, New Forest, Shetland, and the four Welsh breeds, ranging from the beautiful little Section A's to the sturdy big Section D cobs, provide ideal mounts for every type, size and age of young rider. Other countries are not so fortunate. In Europe, Canada and the United States, even very young children have in the past frequently had to ride full-grown horses, but now, in most lands ponies are becoming more

plentiful. Conversely, in Pony Club horse trials nowadays many children compete on horses: quite often their parents' hunters.

In the Middle East, Arabians are largely used. In Hong Kong, ex-racehorses are the mounts not

Left: Lucinda Prior-Palmer, member of the R A Salisbury Plain branch, in 1967. *Below:* Lucinda Green, World and European Gold Medallist, 1987.

Looking, listening and learning can lead to higher things.

Left: 'The Chiddingfold Ride'.

Right: Cyprus.

Left: Jamaica.

Right: Bangkok.

David Green was a member of the Northern Suburbs branch in Australia. *At left* he is seen riding Swift Deal, a 16hh ex-buck jumper from the rodeo circuit who took him from Pony Club trials to the training squad for the Moscow Olympics.

only of adults but also of children. When their racing days are over, the horses are given to selected stables. The problem is that, while a horse may be provided free of charge, its upkeep is extremely expensive – for everything it eats has to be imported.

Bermuda, an island only 22 by 1 miles in size, is a riding stronghold, with all sorts from Shetlands to big horses to ride and a very wide variety of equestrian activities in addition to its Pony Club.

In the Far East there are no Pony Club cross-country competitions – mainly because of the hard ground – but Hong Kong has recently introduced tetrathlons for boys and girls. These exciting competitions have been popular for some time in Canada and the United States.

In the Pony Club Handbook over 100 mounted games and races are listed – and these are the same all over the world. It is fascinating to go to the Mounted Games Study Day. Only then does one realise the enormous variety of games available, the equipment needed, and the necessity of the exact interpretation of the rules. Infinite thought has gone into all of this. The Pony Club-trained child also learns to ride with skill and sympathy while competing in

gymkhanas (for which their ponies should be truly grateful!).

Many overseas countries which have achieved international success have reason to be grateful to the Pony Club for giving their riders a good start. Australian David Green, now married to former World Champion Lucinda Prior-Palmer, came to England in 1971 with a Pony Club team. John Watson and Gerry Sinnott were given the grounding for their success by the Pony Club of Ireland. Mark Todd, Three-Day Event gold medallist in the the Los Angeles Olympics, was a member of the New Zealand Pony Club.

This international aspect of the Pony Club is one of its greatest contributions to sport. To be in a team sent to compete abroad, no matter which country you live in, is the highest reward – not only for performance but for character, too, as every young rider in a team is an ambassador for his or her country.

Since 1980 the Royal Windsor Horse Show has staged a Prince Philip Cup competition for teams from England, Scotland, Wales, Northern Ireland and the Republic of Ireland. The camp for this is on Ascot racecourse and was described to me as 'great fun' – which is probably a masterpiece of understatement.

The Inter-Pacific Rally involves countries bordered by the Pacific Ocean. In 1985 Britain hosted the Rally, providing mounts for and entertaining Pony Club members from Australia, Canada, Hong Kong, Japan, New Zealand and the Philippines.(Unfortunately the cost of this venture and the difficulty of finding suitable mounts for all the riders at a time when their owners were needing them, make it improbable that Britain can repeat such an invitation.)

Members from the UK, the United States and Canada quite often visit each other's countries. One of the earliest of the official visits to Britain was in 1971, when Pony Club riders came from Australia, Canada, Eire, South Africa and the USA.

In 1987 eight Zimbabwians came to Britain to take part in Areas 11 and 13 show jumping and dressage inter-branch competitions, and had the pleasure of jumping at Hickstead on School's Day. In the summer of 1987 Britain sent a team for the first time to the horse trials section of the European Pony Championships, and they returned with bronze medals. It had long puzzled continentals why there had not been representatives in this discipline from Britain – the home

of horse trials – before. As ponies are not allowed to take part in official British Horse Society trials, the Pony Club is the obvious source for such teams. This year they will compete in Denmark.

In 1988 four riders from Britain went all the way to Tasmania to compete in the Australian Bi-Centennial Horse Trials Championships, and enjoyed every minute of their stay. They found the distances and combinations on the cross-country longer and more testing than those to which they were accustomed. 'I think the Aussies go faster than we do,' said one of the riders, 'but their horses are used to it. Most of the competitors were on horse-types, but in Australia a pony is anything up to 14 hands; 14 to 15 hands is a garren; and from 15 hands up is a hack. At first we were expecting to see elegant show horses coming in!' As has been said of England and America: two nations divided by a common language!

The Pony Club is truly a wonderful, worldwide institution – thanks, it must be said, to the dedication of all the adults who started it, developed it and kept it not only running, but ever-growing.

Mark Phillips, a member of the Beaufort branch, competing at area trials in 1963. Twenty-five years later he is still a leading international rider.

The Black Shires of London

Near the centre of London, in the middle of a very busy one-way traffic system, live a flock of geese, some chickens, a rooster, a peacock, a few ducks, a nanny-goat, a ram, two donkeys, a cat, and twenty-three Black Shire horses.

They all live in the stables at the Ram Brewery, Wandsworth, where Young & Co have been brewing beer since 1831. Unlike most breweries these days, Youngs still deliver to their pubs by dray, which is a large, wheeled cart, pulled by two Black Shire horses. Each dray can carry three tons – about twelve full barrels of beer – so the horses have to be big and strong. They also have to be unafraid in heavy traffic, and to learn patience. This takes training.

The horses are bought as three-year olds, completely unbroken, except to a rough halter. They are broken-in over the winter, and then for the rest of the year – until the following spring – these majestic animals spend their time becoming accustomed to noise and traffic, and to

working in pairs. The stable lads lead the young horses through the brewery yard, where there is always plenty of action and noise: large delivery lorries loading up at the keg bay, klaxon hooters blaring, hammering and so on, and behind the stables there is a main road with three lanes of heavy traffic constantly rushing past.

In the spring of his fourth year, a novice horse will be sent out on his first delivery round, with an experienced partner who will help slow down his eagerness to the regulation speed. It can take anything between two and six months for a horse to acquire good road sense.

A brewery horse makes three trips every other day (they work one day, and rest the next), to deliver beer to pubs which are within a three-mile radius of the brewery. There are between twenty and twenty-five pubs in Wandsworth, Putney, Fulham and Chelsea to which the drays deliver. While the draymen unload the barrels of beer, the gentle giants stand patiently, heads in

Rural scene in urban setting.
Left: Bertie and Charlton learning to work as a pair.

nosebags, responding in a friendly manner to any passer-by who cannot resist giving them a pat on the neck.

At any one time there are four pairs on the road, whatever the weather. Unlike lorries, they don't break down and they rarely have accidents. Recently, a careless motorist drove into a dray knocking both draymen to the ground. The horses trotted off – they didn't bolt – and went straight to the nearest pub!

The stables, which are ninety years old, are built on three sides of a square, and inside there are rows of huge stalls, some occupied by the horses whose rest day it is, others by the show horses.

However, the horses don't have the stables all to themselves. The hens and geese, clucking and honking, peck and waddle through the stall lines, unconcerned by the great horses towering over them. In one of the stalls lives a ram, the brewery mascot, and a nanny-goat, while in another there is a pair of donkeys whose annual fixture is to take part in a nativity play at the local hospital. The show horses are excused delivery duties and spend their year visiting all the large agricultural and horse shows such as Horse of the Year, Royal Windsor, Bath & West, South of England, etc.

Peter Tribe, the Head Horseman, has three young horses who he is working up as the brewery's new show team. It will take some years before they reach their peak and then no doubt, they will be adding rosettes to the rows which are already pinned up in the stables. The heavy harness, brasses and blinkers which the show horses wear are all on display in the stables, too. 'It's getting more and more difficult to find good show horses,' says Mr Tribe. 'They are all exported to America, Japan, Germany and Australia, where there is a great demand for them.'

Mr Tribe began his career with horses as a milkman, in the days when some milk rounds were still made by horse and cart. He then worked on a farm, joining the brewery as a stable lad fourteen years ago. He was promoted to Head Horseman (Stable Manager) in 1987. In addition to the ten draymen, he has four lads working in the stables, grooming, feeding, washing down the show horses, polishing the tack, and exercising. There is also a farrier. As you might expect, the roads take their toll on horseshoes. On average, a shoe lasts about four weeks, so the brewery has its own forge and farrier. With twenty-three horses to keep shod, he has to cast about two to three shoes a day.

The age of the Black Shires varies. Constant roadwork proves too much for some of the horses, affecting their joints, so a few may retire at the early age of ten, while others like twenty-year-old Hope, who is a good workhorse, will continue on their rounds until they are twenty or so. The horses are retired to farms, usually as pets, or for showing, and they spend their final years grazing in the countryside – a well-deserved change from the hurly-burly of London streets.

Hercules is an old show horse who still lives at the stables, he refuses to leave!

'He's twenty years old,' says Mr Tribe. 'and he's quite a personality. He makes a great fuss of people and they of him. We don't even have to tie him up. We take him to a show now and then because he loves it. We went to the 1987 Horse of the Year Show and he enjoyed himself immensely.'

This is a way of life which is rapidly disappearing, especially in a huge city. But the Ram Brewery hopes that their Black Shire horses will always continue to be a familiar sight in the streets of south-west London. That is the reason why geese are kept in the stable yard. In 300BC a Roman General called Horatius drove off invaders from Rome by using geese, which can be very fierce. At the Ram Brewery, they say that as long as there are geese in the yard, no other company can take them over, and the gentle, much-loved giants will remain.

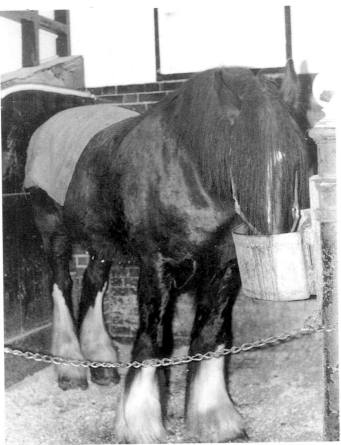

FACT BOX

The ancestors of the Shire horse were the Flemish (Flanders) horse and the Friesian. Both breeds were mostly black in colour. They were crossed with English horses in the mid-17th century when the Fens in East Anglia were being drained to reclaim land for agriculture; big, powerful horses were needed to help with this work. The best Shire horses were bred in Leicestershire, Staffordshire and Derbyshire. They varied in type but had the distinctive feathering on their fetlocks. It was Oliver Cromwell, who came from Huntingdonshire, who gave them the name 'Blacks'.

- Goliath, one of Young and Co's horses, stands at 19.2 hands. He is the largest Shire horse in the UK.

- The average height of the brewery's working horses is 17.3 hands.

- The average weight of the horses is 15-16cwt.

- With a full dray load a pair of Shire horses takes three minutes to accelerate from 0 to 5 miles per hour.

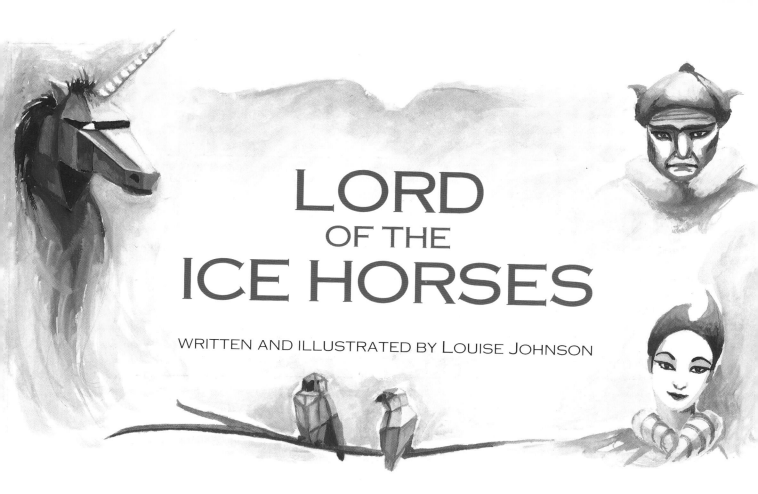

LORD
OF THE
ICE HORSES

WRITTEN AND ILLUSTRATED BY LOUISE JOHNSON

Galaxos, Lord of the Ice Horses, lived in a cave at the edge of the Universe. He had fled there from Earth at the end of the Great Ice Age, when the mighty glaciers crumbled and fell into the sea and warm winds began to blow from the South. He had encased himself in ice and had sped through space in a frozen meteorite, to search the heavens for a place where no-one would find him. He had found the cave at the edge of the universe, shaken the ice from his coat, and trotted inside. It was dark in the cave, but his single horn shimmered with a magic light, and the cave was lit with its soft glow.

Galaxos stared at the stars, and felt deep sadness within him. A single tear fell from one of his deep golden eyes and splashed at his feet. At once a magical ice tree began to grow from the teardrop. As it grew, it bore icy fruit, which ripened and fell to the ground. Other trees sprang up, until the whole cave became an ice forest. A frozen lake spread out from one corner, fed by a frozen waterfall, and ice birds flew among the branches of the trees. But everything was silent except for the sound of Galaxos' hooves

upon the icy ground. Then a gentle wind blew in through the mouth of the cave and sighed amongst the branches of the trees, which glittered in the soft light, and their icy chimes whispered in the air as the breeze touched their branches. Galaxos grew tired of watching the stars. He sighed deeply and walked slowly into the cave.

There he stayed in solitude for nearly a thousand years. Then his loneliness grew too strong for him to resist. He encased himself in ice once more and travelled off towards the nearest stars. He landed on the northern pole of an icy planet. He sniffed the freezing wind and watched the clouds racing across the bright sky. Then he reared on to his haunches and brought his front hooves crashing down upon the frozen ground. Fragments of ice exploded in all directions, and Galaxos' eyes shone and his single horn glowed with a fantastic golden beam of light. Ice horses sprang up from the place where he had stamped his hooves, and he whinnied with joy when he saw them. He reared again and again, crashing his hooves upon the

15

frozen ground and unleashing his magic, until he was surrounded by a herd of ice horses. They milled around him, snorting and stamping and whinnying with joy. Then Galaxos called out to them to follow him, because he was their leader, and they raced off across the frozen wastelands, ice and snow scattering under their hooves, the sun glittering on their icy bodies.

Tales of the beautiful herd of magical horses spread among the people of the planet, until one day they reached the land which lay at the planet's centre. It was ruled over by a powerful

war-lord who dwelt in a huge ice palace.

The war-lord sat in his splendid throne room and mused over the intriguing stories about the herd of magic horses. It was rumoured that the creature who led them was too powerful to be captured. But the war-lord was determined to possess them. He sent for his wizard, Dran and ordered him to work out a plan to ensnare the ice horses.

The wizard Dran was an old man, stiff in his joints and almost deaf. He set up a table in the throne room and placed a crystal ball on it. He peered into the swirling depths of the crystal. Then he mumbled strange words under his long, white beard, and wove mystic symbols in the air with his gnarled old hands. He told the war-lord that the creature was called an 'Isos', a magical, horse-like animal made from the purest crystal. His strength and powers rivalled the war-lord's and he was therefore a threat to the war-lord's domain. The Isos obtained his powers by channelling light through his crystal body into his single horn. If he was to be taken captive his power must be destroyed. This, said Dran, could be done if a chain made from pure Thallium was placed around the creature's neck. However, Dran continued, the Isos would only allow people near him who were pure of heart.

The war-lord commanded Dran to look into the crystal ball once more to search his domain for someone who possessed such noble qualities. The wizard told him that any one of his own three daughters would serve his purpose admirably. The war-lord, delighted at the news, summoned his three daughters to the throne room. They stood demurely before him as he paced up and down wondering which one to choose. Eventually he made his choice: it was to be his middle daughter, the Princess Osar. He knew that she loved horses. Also, she was rather plain, so she was therefore less likely to be of use to him than his other two daughters who were renowned for their beauty.

The war-lord ordered the Princess Osar to search out and bring back the Isos and the rest of the herd. He told her that he had heard of their great beauty and strength and wished to see them for himself. What he did not tell her was that he actually wanted to capture and destroy them. The wizard was set to work to forge the magical Thallium chain. When it was ready, the Princess Osar set off on her journey escorted by a party of her father's warriors.

As soon as they were out of sight, the war-lord commanded his court architect to design and build a massive golden cage with which he would capture the Isos and his herd.

The Princess travelled on for many days across the freezing wastelands. She sat huddled in a sleigh pulled by a pure white polar bear. She was wrapped in furs which she held tightly up to her chin, against the icy winds which taunted her with their freezing fingers.

The little group passed through harsh granite mountains and along the green depths of glaciers. The only sounds that accompanied them were the whistling wind, the crunching of snow, and the swish of the sleigh.

Then one morning the Princess saw faint shapes moving in the distance. They glinted in the sunlight and the wind carried the sounds of their stamping hooves and whinneyings. She had found the Isos and his herd. The little band crept towards them cautiously, and by the afternoon were quite close to the herd.

The Princess climbed out of the sleigh and, carrying the magical chain, walked slowly towards them. Galaxos lifted his head. His golden eyes shone. Walking towards him was a human whose heart was pure and kind, without the fear and malice that he had seen in others. The Princess smiled at Galaxos. He was so majestic and he had an aura of quiet strength. She stretched out her hand towards him. He nuzzled her gently and she kissed him on his warm nose. Then she innocently slipped the chain around his neck. Her father had told her that the chain was a gift to the Isos. He had not mentioned its magical powers. She talked quietly to Galaxos, and told him of her father's desire to meet him. Galaxos trusted her and agreed to return with her to the palace. He did not realise that his powers were being drained by the chain around his neck. His ice horses followed nervously behind him, tossing their heads and rolling their eyes. On the return journey, the Princess and Galaxos talked about many things, and a deep bond of friendship formed between them.

Many days later they reached the palace. The war-lord's heralds warned of their approach, and the palace bustled with activity. The Princess's sleigh moved into the central courtyard, above which the huge golden cage, now completed, slowly swung. Galaxos followed her, surrounded by his ice horses whose icy hooves clattered nervously on the freezing cobble-stones. Warriors of the war-lord followed behind them at a discreet distance, but blocking their escape.

In the gateway at the other end of the courtyard the war-lord was waiting. He called to the Princess to join him. Once she had reached his side he raised his hand, as if in salute to Galaxos, but it was actually a signal to cut the rope that was holding up the huge cage. It came crashing down over the frightened horses, who

reared in panic and crashed their hooves against the bars. But it was too late. They were trapped.

Galaxos was in a great fury at the war-lord's treachery, and he gathered his strength to destroy the war-lord and his palace. But his powers had gone. The golden light vanished from his eyes and from his horn, and he hung his head as the force that gave him life was sucked from him. Slowly he began to die. He sank to his knees, his breath rasping in his throat. The ice horses began to die, too. One by one they fell to the cobble-stones and started to melt back into the ice from which they had been formed.

Galaxos looked at the Princess with his sightless eyes. She stood beside her father. Tears streamed down her cheeks as she sobbed with horror and shock at her friend's anguish. Her father chuckled, and patted her on the back. 'Well done, Osar', he said, 'Well done'. She turned and fled. Galaxos stared after her with a deep sadness in his heart.

Back in her room, the Princess cried ceaselessly. She could not believe her father's

treachery. He had lied to her. He was now feasting in the throne room whilst Galaxos lay dying. She could see him at the centre of the cage, his body glinting in the moonlight. All of the ice horses had gone. She ran from her room and crept into the courtyard. Her father had not bothered to post a guard, he was so sure of his success.

She slipped through the bars of the cage, and walked slowly towards Galaxos' body. He lay perfectly still, but she could hear his shallow breath. She cradled his icy head in her arms, 'I'm sorry, I'm sorry,' she whispered in despair. A tear fell from her cheek and splashed on to his face. Slowly he opened his eyes. 'Please take off the chain,' he whispered.

She took the chain from around his neck. He lay there for some time, his breathing faint, and for a moment she thought he had died. Then a miracle began to happen. A golden light spread from the tip of his horn down into his body. He opened his eyes and they began to glow, until they were too bright to look at. He climbed to his feet, lifted his head, and let out a roar of anger. The air around his body shimmered with energy, and his horn pulsed with a rainbow of light. Suddenly a beam of energy shot from the horn, and the cage disintegrated.

Galaxos galloped into the palace, sparks flying from his hooves. People ran in terror from him as he rampaged through the halls and corridors. At last he reached the throne room and stood before the cowering war-lord. The war-lord called upon his wizard to defend him, but Dran took one look at Galaxos and ran off in the opposite direction as fast as his wizened old legs would carry him.

Galaxos stood before the war-lord, and his eyes glowed with anger. 'Thus I punish you,' he cried in his deep, rich voice, 'for killing my ice horses, and using your innocent daughter to capture me.' He touched the war-lord with his glowing horn, and in seconds the terrified tyrant was transformed from flesh and blood to a lifeless statue of pure ice. Then Galaxos turned and galloped from the collapsing palace.

The Princess Osar stood forlornly in the courtyard. Galaxos came thundering towards her. He stood before her, his eyes glowing. Then he said gently: 'Come with me to my beautiful ice cave at the edge of the universe.' Osar smiled, and climbed on to his strong back. He encased them both in ice and sped off into the mists of space.

Fit for Anything

Karen Bush

How often do you ride? And for how long? If your time on board a pony is limited (you may have exams to study for; it may be winter and too dark to ride in the evenings; or you may not have a pony at all and have to wait for a weekly lesson) you'll find that a lot of time is wasted. *Wasted,* that is, in the sense that you may be spending an awful lot of time merely loosening off. Just when your stiffnesses have worn off and you are all ready to settle down to more serious work, you may find that Snowy is too shattered, or the lesson has come to an end!

But don't despair. There are lots of exercises which you can do without a pony when you have a spare minute, and which will keep you fit, supple and ready for action the next time you are in the saddle. Anyway, if you have particular problems when you are riding you may find that by concentrating on some exercises it will even help you to overcome them.

The fitter you are, the better. After all, you won't be of much use to Snowy if you collapse on his neck in a puffing heap after just a short spell of sitting trot or canter!

You might feel that you've grown out of *skipping.* But in fact it is a really good way of getting fit; lots of boxers as well as event riders use it in their training programmes. Not only will it make you fitter, but it will also improve your co-ordination and sharpen up your reflexes.

Cycling (especially up hills) is also good: particularly if you don't sit on the saddle. If you feel rather hot after all that exertion, try a nice cool dip at your local swimming pool. As well as being fun, *swimming* will increase your lung capacity considerably. Of course, if you find all this too easy, you could always try skipping underwater instead!

Now to deal with particular exercises for each part of you body. Concentrate on those which help you most.

Starting at the top, you can relieve tension in your neck by dropping your chin forward on to your chest (but don't slouch) and rolling your head slowly from side to side. It helps if you imagine yourself arching your neck like a pony when he is accepting the bit.

Next, make some chewing movements with your mouth. You'd be surprised at how often you grit your teeth when concentrating hard on something, and how much it can make the rest of you stiff!

Working your way downwards, hunch your shoulders right up beneath your ears, and then shrug them backwards and downwards. Circle

each arm backwards in turn – not forwards, or you'll undo all the good and become round-shouldered and tense again.

Let your hands go floppy, then wiggle them about on the ends of your wrists in both up-and-down and side-to-side movements. This will keep them supple, rather than fixed and unyielding. A good exercise to keep fingers supple is to tap them in turn on top of a desk or working surface. It will increase your ability to co-ordinate their movements, so that you will be able to use two pairs of reins easily, and will be more tactful when using just one pair. Learning to play the

these to start with, or you will feel as though Snowy has just kicked you in the stomach!

Last, but not least – your legs. Hands up anyone who has trouble mounting! This exercise will be especially useful for those who do. Put one foot on a chair in front of you, keeping the other foot at right angles to your body. Slowly lean forward over your raised foot, and then straighten

piano or a wind instrument can also help with this, and has an extra bonus in that it develops an invaluable sense of rhythm.

Having stretched and loosened off the top part of your body, you can begin to turn your attention to your middle. Hold both arms out to either side at shoulder height, palms uppermost. Stand with your feet spread comfortably apart and your arms in a straight line with each other. Swivel the top half of your body first to the left, and then to the right. But keep your hips square to your feet, though. No cheating!

Another 'waist' exercise also needs to be done while you are standing up. Spread your feet apart as before, then slide your hand as far down the side of your leg as you can reach. Remember to do this an equal number of times on each side, or you will become one-sided and crooked when riding.

While you are still feeling energetic, try a few sit-ups to strengthen your stomach muscles. You'll need to ask someone to hold your feet. Lie down, fold your arms, and then sit up. Lie down again slowly, and keep your arms folded. It sounds easy enough, but don't do too many of

up again. A word of warning here – if you are using the furniture at home, remember to remove your muddy boots before you start!

A nice, easy exercise to supple up ankles is to sit down and circle both feet in either direction. If you have problems trying to keep your heels from shooting upwards while you are riding, a really beneficial exercise for you is the 'alternative' press-up. Don't be put off by the name. They aren't as difficult as the usual sort! Stand at arm's length away from the wall, with your arms held out straight in front of you, palms resting on the surface. Bend your elbows and slowly lean forward until your nose nearly touches the wall. Keep your heels flat on the floor.

When trying out these exercises, bear in mind that a little each day will help – but overdoing it will make you ache and more likely to stiffen up. Little and often is the thing to remember. Then even if you only get the chance to ride at weekends, you might one day end up in the same sort of class as Chris Bartle or Jennie Loriston-Clarke. Well almost. Miracles don't happen overnight!

Howlers

This competitor is jumping the practice jump before the Pony Club Show Jumping Finals. She was not allowed to compete – for 16 errors of turnout. What are they?

Answers are on page 63.

Never Give In

Toni Webber

Sometimes Jo wondered whether it was really worth it. Today, for example. Standing on the windswept common, shoulders hunched and collar turned up against the sudden flurries of needle-like raindrops, she was more than ready to turn her back on the whole proceedings and trek homewards. She breathed into the inside of her gloves to warm her frozen fingers, and wished that the practice would come to an end.

'Come on Jo. For goodness sake, wake up!' Mrs Ansty's strong, often shrill, voice penetrated her misery, and Jo realised that they'd finished the Bottle Race, which she wasn't in, and were about to start practising the Old Sock Race, which she was.

'Old Nasty's in a real paddy today,' murmured Clare as Jo urged Pickles into place.

'So would you be if you had such a feeble lot to deal with,' said Mrs Ansty sharply. 'Don't you want to get to the Zone finals this year?'

Yes, they did, Jo reflected. They wanted to get to the Zone and they wanted to get to Wembley, although the latter seemed rather a forlorn hope. They particularly wanted to beat the West team, who had been their special rivals ever since the branch had split into two some ten years before.

This year, for the first time, they had a really promising Prince Philip Cup squad. Instead of having two or three moderately good people and half a dozen rabbits, there were seven or eight strong contenders for the first team. They had practised at least once weekly all through the winter, and now, with the Area competition just a week away, Mrs Ansty had them on the common every day. Nobody's place was assured, she had told them firmly.

East were sending two teams to the Area finals, and Mrs Ansty was determined that the A team would qualify for the Zone. Jo and Pickles, her games pony, had been in the A team for the last four years. This year was Jo's last chance to make the Zone. Next year, she would be too old.

But Mrs Ansty's hectoring manner made Jo feel resentful. After all, she and Pickles knew what to do. They'd been at it long enough. There was no need for Nasty to shout at *her*.

Now it was her turn. She urged Pickles forward to the start line and leaned forward to receive the sock from the incoming rider's outstretched hand. Another flurry of ice-cold raindrops hit Pickles in the face and he backed off just as Clare reached out to Jo. The sock slipped from their numb fingers and rolled on the ground. Quick as a flash, Clare leapt from her pony, retrieved the sock, handed it to Jo, and Pickles was away.

Hardly checking Pickles's stride as they reached the bucket, Jo bent down over his shoulder to drop the sock into the container. But the rain made her misjudge the distance and the

sock caught the rim of the bucket and bounced out. Jo was out of the saddle in an instant. She replaced the sock and vaulted back on.

Gallop to the other end. Off Pickles. Running hard for some yards before the change-over line. Grab a sock. Turn Pickles round and vault on him again even as his head turns for home. . .

That had been her intention. But it wasn't her day, and she missed her vault, so that she had to check Pickles and steady the plunging pony before she could get safely back into the saddle. This had always been a risk. Pickles was immensely fast and – provided his rider could keep up with him – he was one of the best games specialists in the country. But if things went wrong, thought Jo ruefully, it would be a bit of a problem.

'Well, that was awful,' said Mrs Ansty crossly as the game finished. 'Come on, we'll do it again.'

By the time the last race was under way, there was open hostility between the games squad and their determined trainer. The rain was now beating down hard, and in the Five-Flag Race everything went wrong. Riders picked up two flags at once, fumbled the change-overs, knocked cones over, circled the receiving cone two or three times before slotting the flag into place.

'There's not much point in entering if you're going to be as bad as this,' said Mrs Ansty as she called it a day. 'And it's no good complaining about the rain. We could have even worse weather at the Area on Saturday. . . Right then, same time tomorrow. And Jo, you'll have to control Pickles better than you did today or you won't even make the B team.'

She turned away, and Jo pulled a face at her back. 'Don't let her get to you,' said Clare soothingly as she and Jo hacked home across the common. 'Of course you'll be in the A team. You're easily the best.'

'I wasn't the best today,' said Jo gloomily, trying to steady the jogging Pickles to a walk. 'Where does this pony get his energy? You'd think he'd be exhausted after such a morning.'

'It's what makes him so good,' observed Clare. Her own pony, Holly, was a steady dependable sort, not particularly fast but a good anchor in a Prince Philip team. The girls lived next door to each other and kept their ponies in a nearby field.

Back home, they rubbed the ponies down and turned them out. Both ponies selected a fine

muddy spot, sank down and rolled, before
making their way to the water trough with their
coats nicely plastered with mud. The girls hung
haynets in a sheltered spot and the ponies
settled down to eat, their tails spread out against
their quarters to protect them from the rain.

In Jo's kitchen, thawing their frozen hands
round steaming mugs of tea, the girls moaned to
Jo's mother about the dreaded Mrs Ansty.

'I've a good mind to tell old Nasty what she
can do with her A team,' Jo finished. 'Mounted
games are supposed to be *fun.*'

'I thought you wanted to win, Jo' said her
mother mildly.

'Well, yes,' admitted Jo.

'Would you say you are better now than you
were before Mrs Ansty took over the training?'

'Oh, heaps better,' said Clare.

'There you are then,' said Jo's mother. 'Mrs
Ansty wants you to *win*. She's very strong-willed
and she works hard. She sets high standards and
she expects you to come up to them.'

'She could be nicer about it,' muttered Jo a
little sullenly. 'I mean, it was really cold up on
the common today, and when your hands are cold
it's easy to make mistakes. *She* seemed to think
we weren't trying.'

'And I daresay you all got bad-tempered
yourselves and answered her back.' Jo's mother
poured herself a second mug of tea and looked at
her daughter over the rim.

'Well, everyone knows that Jo is the best in
the team.' said Clare. 'Pickles is such a brilliant
gymkhana pony.'

'Pickles may be brilliant, but he can't do the
games by himself. Don't forget that Pickles is
only as good as his rider.' Jo's mother gathered
up the mugs and put them on the draining
board. 'Anyway, think about it. Never give in.
When is the team selection being made?'

'After tomorrow's practice.'

As she hung over the gate that evening, giving
the ponies their late-night carrots, Jo considered
her mother's advice.

With typical April inconsistency, the rain had
stopped, the wind was barely enough to ruffle the
burgeoning leaves, and a bright moon peered
down from a star-laden sky.

It was certainly true, thought Jo, that
everyone had improved since old Nasty had taken
over the training. There was a sharpness about
the team that hadn't been there before: a feeling
that, with a little bit of luck, there was nothing
they could not do, no opponent they could not
beat.

And if she were really honest, old Nasty wasn't
old Nasty all the time. Sometimes she could be
quite nice. She didn't waste time blaming you if
you made a mistake during a competition – not if
you were really doing your best.

Perhaps it *was* a bit wimpish to give in just
because someone felt you should be working a
little harder. Even worse – Jo shuddered at the
thought – supposing she packed it in or got
dropped or something, and the team went
through to the Zone without her. That really
would be a complete waste of the past four years,
and she wouldn't get a second chance. Never give
in, her mother had said, never give in.

'Are you going to tell Mrs Ansty that you don't
want to be in the team?' asked Clara as they
made their way out of the gate and along the
bridleway that led to the common. It was a much
milder day today. Jo thought she could probably
discard her anorak once they reached the
practice ground.

'Let's see how the practice goes first,' said Jo.

The sun seemed to have a benefical effect on
everyone. Mrs Ansty was in a positively beamish
mood, and they ran through the seven races,
including the warm-up, with hardly a mistake.

'Do that on Saturday,' said Mrs Ansty at the end, 'and we're sure to make the Zone. We might even beat the Wests! Well done, all of you.'

The riders waited, dismounting to give the ponies' backs a rest, knowing that Mrs Ansty's next words would reveal their fate – A team, B team or just reserve and a hope for the future.

'These are the teams.' Mrs Ansty read through the list of names. She paused when she came to Jo's. 'I'm making you the A team captain, Jo. That is, if you're still quite happy to be in the team.'

Jo blushed. Had old Nasty been reading her thoughts? And was there a hint of a smile on her face?

'Thanks, Mrs Ansty. Of course I'll be in the team. Whatever made you think I wouldn't?'

'Right,' said Mrs Ansty. 'Same time tomorrow, rain or snow. We've three more practices before the Area. Don't be late.'

Jo couldn't be absolutely sure, but she was almost certain that Mrs Ansty winked.

Accumulator Stakes

A Game for Two Teams or Two Players and a Question-master/Judge

10 questions for 10 jumps. Each question answered successfully scores the allotted number of points. Unanswered questions, or those answered incorrectly score nothing, *but* the judge must give the correct answer. The highest score is the winner.

Judge's Answers on Page 63. No Riding on the Course First!

Team or Individual A

		Points
1.	How many inches in a hand?	10
2.	What is the chestnut or castor?	20
3.	What is a Morgan?	30
4.	What is a unicorn?	40
5.	What colour is a Suffolk Punch?	50
6.	What is a hamstring?	60
7.	Who was John Frederick Herring?	70
8.	What happens at Badminton and in what month of the year?	80
9.	What was the name of Napoleon's charger?	90
10.	What is sweet itch?	100
Cross out faults		Total

Team or Individual B

		Points
1.	Where is the frog?	
2.	What is the ergot?	
3.	What is a Standardbred?	10
4.	What is a pickaxe?	20
5.	What colour is a Hafflinger?	30
6.	What is a stringhalt?	40
7.	Who was George John Whyte-Melville?	50
8.	What happens at Burghley and in what month of the year?	60
9.	What was the name of El Cid's great white warhorse?	70
10.	What is laminitis?	80
		90
Cross out faults		100
		Total

J.S.

Snap Happy
Kit Houghton

Photographing horses can be rewarding as well as good fun. But have you sometimes wondered why a picture of your favourite pony makes him look rather like a giraffe? Or, if your pony is jumping, why the picture is all blurred? Here are a few tips which will help you to avoid some of the mistakes that most beginners make.

If your camera is the 'instamatic' type – that is, with a fixed-focus lens and no shutter-speed dial – the options are limited. Your action pictures can never be very good; and to fill the picture with a jumping subject will mean standing too close to the fence for safety. But all is not lost. There are many poses which can be caught while your pony is stationary.

Firstly the 'classic' pose. For this you should stand at 90 degrees to the subject, mid-way between the head and the tail. Make sure that the hind leg furthest from you is in front of the other hind leg which should be nearly vertical. The forelegs should have a small gap between them, with the foreleg furthest from you slightly behind the other foreleg. Before standing your pony up it is most important to check the background. Nothing looks worse than posts or trees 'growing out' from behind your subject. Choose the brow of a hill, where the background will just be sky, or some flat ground with a fence or hedge some distance away.

To make your pony seem taller, crouch down a little. But don't lie on the ground, or he will seem to be all legs and no body. You must keep your pony alert so that his ears are pricked when the photograph is taken. Have someone to help you do this by waving a cloth, rustling a bag or turning a radio on. A bucket of food is not a good idea as the pony will tend to go towards it. Be careful not to frighten your pony, or he'll be off!

For good pictures you will need more sophisticated equipment – preferably a camera with adjustable shutter speeds and a zoom lens. The best speed for 'freezing' a fast-moving subject is 1/500th of a second. The other technique to learn is 'panning' the camera with the subject. To do this, follow the subject as it moves past you, and at the height of the action

The 'classic' pose.

A low angle on the take-off side of a
fence can be very effective.

This picture is rather distracting, with
the trees in the background.

An unusual angle can make for an
interesting picture.

Taken at sunset. The pony's head and foreleg is silhouetted by the sun.

A frosty morning. By taking this picture against the sun the horse stands out against the background, and shows up the frost on the ground.

Racehorses taken with a slow shutter speed (1/30th second) to give the impression of speed. Remember to try and find bright colours, as this helps to emphasise the speed.

Left: Different views of a gymkhana. Always be on the look-out for unusual or amusing pictures.

Below: Horses jumping out of water, with the spray around them, can make very spectacular pictures.

take the picture. It is best to practise this without film in the camera as it can become very expensive!

Imagine a horse jumping a fence. Position yourself just in front of and at an angle of 45 degrees to the fence – and a safe distance away. With your zoom lens, adjust the size of the fence in the picture by altering the zoom control on the lens. Make sure that the fence almost fills the viewfinder. As the pony approaches the fence, follow it with your camera. Press the shutter as the pony leaves the ground and continue to follow through until the pony has landed. In this way the camera will be following the subject, and the picture that you will have taken will be sharp.If you want to give the impression of movement, select a slow shutter speed (1/30th of a second) and then pan, as described above. This will

Right: Bobbing for apples. Don't forget to get down to the same level as the subject.

Below: Catching the action at Pony Club mounted games.

Above: Strong shapes against the sun, make this an ideal subject for a black and white picture.

Left: Mark Todd's Olympic horse, Charisma, caught in an unusual pose.

produce a picture with all sorts of interesting blurrs and lines, giving an impression of great speed.

Don't get too carried away by photographing obvious subjects. Try to look around for more off-beat and amusing pictures. At an event or a show interesting subjects can often be seen in the collecting or horsebox lines. Try to keep the picture simple and not too cluttered. Always try to get as close to your subject as possible, as there is nothing worse than a dot on the landscape.

These days most people use colour film, but black and white can be very interesting if you make use of form and shape. It is essential to keep practising, and to have your camera always handy; the more familiar you become with it, the more likely you will be to catch those fleeting moments.

Opposite above: A straightforward jumping picture, but with lots of colour on both rider and the crowd behind to make the picture vibrant.

Opposite below: A very low angle which makes the fence look enormous. But don't try lying in the ditch yourself: this was taken with a camera operated by remote control.

Above: Racehorses exercising on the beach. Try taking pictures in different locations.

Right: Contrasting colours of a horse standing in a field of oil seed rape. Don't forget to ask the farmer's permission!

Playing Hard to Get

March 16

Dad said that he might as well sell Frosty because I never spend any time riding him these days. It took me ages to persuade him to buy me a pony for Christmas and if he does sell Frosty I'll never be able to make him think it's a good idea to buy me another one. It isn't as though I don't want to ride him – I just can't catch him! He never used to be like that until recently. I used to ride him every day. I'll really miss him if he goes.

March 17

I told my friend Jane what Dad had said about selling Frosty. Apparently her pony used to be exactly the same. She suggested that instead of riding him each time I caught him, I simply should give him a small feed, groom him and then turn him back into the field again. I did point out that I can't get close enough even to wave a feed bucket under his nose – let alone groom him. But she said just to be patient and persevere. She reckons that once he has realised that he gets something nice whenever he is caught, he won't be any problem to catch after a while. Mind you: it'll mean that I'll have to visit a couple of times a day, not just when I want to ride.

March 18

Dad was talking today about putting an advert for Frosty in the local paper. I told him about Jane's theory – that maybe Frosty didn't enjoy going for long rides as much as I do. Dad finally agreed to give Jane's plan a try before making a final decision about Frosty's fate. I put the

campaign into action right away this evening. I made a really tasty feed and took it down to the field. I still couldn't get near him. I had to leave the bucket in the middle of the paddock. Then I retreated to the gate to watch. He seemed to enjoy his supper, although he did keep a rather suspicious eye on me over the top of the bucket!

March 25

I can get much closer to Frosty now than I could before: but still not close enough to catch him. This evening Jane decided to come with me in case she could help – and she actually succeeded in capturing him. I don't know who was more surprised: I or Frosty. Jane squatted down by the bucket and waited until he couldn't bear it any longer and wandered over to see what we had brought for him. He was very suspicious at first, and stood as far away as possible, stretching his nose out towards the feed. When Jane didn't make a move he became more confident and moved closer. Jane straightened up very slowly and rustled a piece of paper she had in her pocket. This really got him interested – and before he knew what was happening, Jane had slipped the lead rope around his neck. We gave him a titbit as a reward, and a good grooming. Then we turned him out with his headcollar on so that it will be easier to catch hold of him next time.

March 26
I was actually able to catch Frosty today on my own – the first time in ages! I went though the same routine as yesterday. Stangely enough, he seems far less grumpy than he used to be. I'm even beginning to enjoy my early morning trips to see him (though its an effort to get out of bed). He actually seems pleased to see me, and has started waiting by the gate.

April 10
Went for the most wonderful ride today with Frosty and Jane. Her pony is a terrific jumper, and she says she is really looking forward to taking him to some shows this summer. If I want to go, she has offered to take Frosty in the trailer with her pony. I'm sure Frosty will be brilliant in the gymkhana classes. It's funny how well you can get to know a pony without having to ride him. I notice so much more about Frosty's moods now that I spend some time with him instead of just riding.

April 15
Jane suggested that now Frosty is so good about being caught I should leave his headcollar off when he goes back out into the field. She's right really. Even though it is a good fit, it could still be dangerous if it got caught on anything.

April 20
The first show schedules arrived this morning. Dad is really keen on the idea and even paid my entry fees. He seems to have changed his mind about selling Frosty.

April 25
Disaster! I couldn't catch Frosty again today – and yet he has been so good lately. Jane thinks that it might be due to the fact that the grass is early this year, and although Frosty is quite greedy he is more interested in the grazing than in the feeds I bring him. We decided that the best thing to do is move him on to a paddock which has less grass. He is so fat anyway that it won't do him any harm to lose weight. It would be awful if he got laminitis or tendon trouble through being fat.

April 27
Frosty is fine about being caught again now he is in a barer field – although I'm sure he doesn't really approve! Not long to the show now: just four days.

April 30
Jane offered to let me keep Frosty in one of her spare stables overnight, so that he won't get all covered in grass stains after I've shampooed him. I had a few problems in catching him again. For some reason he decided that it was more fun to gallop round the field, chasing the other ponies. Dad tried to help me round him up, but he just got more and more excited. Then we tried to corner him, holding a lunge line between us to form a kind of fence. Unfortunately it didn't work very well with only two of us, and we kept cornering the wrong pony. Luckily Jane arrived and came to find out what the delay was, just as we were about to give up and Dad was threatening to sell Frosty for glue. She said it was just naughtiness and excitement, and that chasing him was only going to make him worse. She then caught the other three ponies and left Dad and me holding them outside the field gate. Once his friends had gone, Frosty looked really disappointed, and she caught him without any trouble at all. I left him all tucked up for the night with a nice thick straw bed, and looking very sheepish.

May 1
We won our first rosette together today. Dad won't hear a word said against Frosty now. I think he'd rather sell *me!*

Spot the Difference

There are 10 differences between the 2 pictures

Answers are on page 63.

A Helping Hand

Judith Draper

In October 1930 a British Army officer named Geoffrey Brooke was posted to Egypt to command the Cavalry Brigade. Brigadier (later Major-General) Brooke was not only a distinguished soldier, he was also a fine horseman and had been a regular member of the British show jumping team in the 1920s. His wife, Dorothy, also a great lover of horses, accompanied him to Heliopolis, just outside Cairo. Although no one knew it at the time, Dorothy Brooke's journey was to have far-reaching effects upon the lives of hundreds of thousands of horses and donkeys in Egypt.

Mrs Brooke knew that at the end of the 1914-18 war more than 20,000 horses who had served with the Army in Palestine had been sold by the British to Egyptian owners. Why were they not taken home to England with the soldiers? 'Lack of transport' was one excuse given by the authorities, though it seems more likely that it was simply less trouble for everyone to leave them where they were. In fact, it would have been kinder to have shot them all there and then.

The appalling condition of working horses and donkeys in Egypt's hot climate horrified Mrs Brooke. Most were weakened by years of inadequate food and water. Lame, crippled, and with open sores caused by ill-fitting harness, they struggled under the whip, day and night to please their masters. Mrs Brooke decided that the time had come to seek out and rescue any surviving British Army horses – they could easily be recognised by their distinctive brands.

With the assistance of her husband and a small group of other sympathetic people, she spent the next few years searching for and buying up every pathetic old war horse she could find. The money was donated by people in Britain after English newspapers published letters from Mrs Brooke begging for help.

Tracking down the horses was extremely difficult work, for they were scattered over a wide area. Also, Egyptian men were not used to doing business with a woman! Finding stables to use as a base was another great problem. But Mrs Brooke was determined to succeed and in the end she overcame even what seemed to be the most impossible difficulties.

A worn-out old horse outside the clinic in Alexandria.

By the time she arrived in Egypt, the British Army horses were more than twenty years old and in a state of near collapse. For all except a small handful who were strong enough to stand the long journey to England, the kindest end to their suffering was humane destruction. However, upon arrival at Mrs Brooke's Cairo stables, horses who were not in too much pain were first given a few days' 'holiday', with plentiful food, water, bedding and kind handling – things which they had not known for many years.

When eventually she was satisfied that she had tracked down all the Army horses who were still alive – 5,000 were found – Mrs Brooke might well have believed that she had done enough. But her experiences among the poor people of Egypt had presented her with an even greater chance to help animals. She realised that all working equines in the country desperately needed help. As a result, she decided to turn her stables into a free veterinary clinic for those people too poor to pay for treatment for their animals. Thus it came about that the Old War Horse Memorial Hospital, now known as the Brooke Hospital for

Donkeys straining to pull a heavy load into the Zebaline camp in the Mokattam hills, Cairo.

Animals, Cairo, was opened in 1934. The road in which the stables stand – in one of Cairo's poorest areas – later became known as 'the Street of the English Lady'.

Today, more than fifty years later, the work of the Brooke Hospital continues to grow. In addition to the well-equipped hospital in Cairo, there are small clinics in Alexandria, Luxor and Aswan. Using mobile clinic vans sent out from England, the vets are able to visit markets and villages further afield and to collect injured animals. Recently the hospital opened its first clinic outside Egypt – at the tourist centre of Petra, in Jordan. Much valuable work is being done at all these places by the hospital's devoted staff.

It is easy for Europeans to criticise people in Middle Eastern countries; to call them cruel and heartless. Of course, some owners are deliberately cruel – this is the same everywhere in the world. But all too often the animals' suffering is caused by ignorance which itself is the result of poverty. In Egypt there is poverty of a kind unimaginable to most Westerners.

Take, for example, the group of people known as the Zebaline. They are modern Cairo's dustmen, who have to work in this huge city without the help of modern machinery. With their primitive two-wheeled carts, usually drawn by three donkeys, they roam the city collecting rubbish. Back at the rubbish tips they sort out anything which can be eaten for themselves or their animals, and anything which can be sold for re-cycling, such as paper. Because they have nowhere else to go, they build themselves ramshackle homes among the rubbish, and there they live with their children, goats, pigs, chickens, dogs and donkeys (horses are not tough enough for this work and are rarely seen among the Zebaline). Often the Zebaline live without electricity or running water and in the most filthy conditions. Little wonder, then, that the donkeys suffer all sorts of injuries and ailments: everything from broken knees and infected harness galls to worms and tetanus.

Zebaline children, who start work driving donkey carts at a very early age, have no Pony Club to teach them how to care for their animals. They learn by watching their parents, and their parents tend to be hopelessly ignorant about animal welfare. To a European horse owner, it may sound simple common sense, but to many poor, ill-educated Egyptians it comes as a complete surprise, to be told that an animal will work better if it is adequately fed and watered, correctly shod and harnessed, given some rest and shade from the fierce sun and not beaten incessantly; or that old Egyptian 'treatments' such as cutting off the tops of a donkey's ears will not cure it of anything but will almost certainly cause the unfortunate creature to contract tetanus. Until the Brooke Hospital's vets began making regular visits to the rubbish tips a few years ago and began vaccinating the animals, the average life of a Zebaline donkey was only four years.

Slowly, things are improving. Owners are beginning to learn that it is better to ask the vet to look at their sick or injured animal before it is too late. The hospital still provides all treatment free of charge, and it provides a small amount of compensation towards the cost of a new animal to any owner whose horse or donkey needs to be put down. Most importantly, the vets take every opportunity to teach owners the basics of good horsemanship. The nice thing is that once an Egyptian owner has learned how to care for his animal he takes great pride in it. It is, after all, his most valuable possession. Without a horse or donkey, many a poor Egyptian could not work, and if he could not work he would starve. Nowadays more and more proud owners can be seen polishing their harness, cart, and well-kept horse at every available opportunity.

Unfortunately, although the standard of horse care is gradually improving, the number of road accidents involving horses and donkeys ensures that the hospital stables are always full. The streets of Cairo and Alexandria are bursting at the seams with traffic, and all Egyptians seem to drive too fast. When there is a crash, it is a horse or donkey who so often comes off worst. Broken limbs are commonplace. Sending to the Brooke Hospital for help can take hours, since there are no public telephone boxes in Egypt.

True to Mrs Brooke's wishes, those animals brought into the hospital for destruction who are not in too much pain are given a short holiday before they are put down. It is touching to see worn-out animals relaxing, perhaps for the first time in their lives, on a deep straw bed, or enjoying the unheard-of luxury of eating and drinking as much as they want.

Perhaps those 20,000 British Army horses did not suffer in vain. If it had not been for them there might never have been a Brooke Hospital. And without a Brooke Hospital, more than a quarter of a million other horses and donkeys would have spent miserable lives with no hope of veterinary care.

The Brooke Hospital runs a Junior Supporters' Club. Anyone under the age of 18 can join. It costs £2.00 per year. For details write to Richard Searight (Dorothy Brooke's grandson) at the following address:

Brooke Hospital for Animals (JCAR),
1 Regent Street, London SW1Y 4PA.

A gharry horse enjoying a drink at the Luxor clinic trough.

Pair Them Up

Pair a lettered picture with a numbered picture.
What horse term does each pair depict?

Answers are on page 63.

To Catch a Thief

Kate Robertson

'I don't believe it!' exclaimed Mr Patterson, looking up from his newspaper.

'What don't you believe?' asked his wife, who was sitting opposite him at the breakfast table.

'It says here in the local newspaper that there are rustlers in the district.'

'Rustlers! Here? I thought they only existed in the old Wild West,' said Jane, his daughter, as she spread far too much marmalade on her toast and crammed it into her mouth.

'You shouldn't put so much food into your mouth at once,' said Mr Patterson. 'No. I'm afraid rustling still goes on, and in England, too. However in this case they seem to be stealing tack, especially new or expensive saddles. According to the newspaper there have been three cases round here in the last fortnight.'

'That's beastly of them,' said Jane, who loved horses and had a pony of her own. She felt great sympathy for the people whose saddles had been stolen. 'They had better not steal Misty's saddle or I shall . . .'

'Or you'll what?' interrupted her twin brother, Charles, who liked to be precise about things.

'Oh I don't know what I'd do,' said Jane angrily. 'It would be so awful if I couldn't ride Misty, especially as the gymkhana is in two days' time.'

'Now then,' said Mrs Patterson. 'There's no need to jump the gun, children. I'm sure that the thieves wouldn't be interested in Misty's old saddle. But just to be on the safe side we'll ask Daddy to check the padlock on the tackroom door.'

'I'll do it this evening,' promised Mr Patterson. 'Now I must get off to work. What are you two children up to today?'

'I'm riding Misty over to Fiona's,' said Jane. 'We're going to practise jumping in her field.' Fiona Steele was Jane's best friend and she lived on the farm at the other end of their village.

'I think I'll come with you,' said Charles. 'I've heard that Mr Steele has got a new tractor and I'd love to have a look at it.'

'Well that's fine,' said Mrs Patterson, relieved that Charles wouldn't be spending all day in his room, playing games on his computer. 'Just make sure that you're both back for lunch.'

It was a lovely summer's day when the twins set out for the farm. Birds were singing in the hedgerows and honey bees were buzzing about their business in the still, quiet air. Misty's hooves made dainty clopping noises on the road and every now and then she swished her tail or twisted her head towards the overhanging branches, breaking off a delicious mouthful of greenery.

Jane thought that Misty was a wonderful pony. She was nearly 14 hands, and her coat was the colour of light fudge. Although she misbehaved every now and then, especially at Pony Club rallies, Jane forgave her, because it was just high spirits.

Charles walked beside them, deep in thought. He was thinking how wonderful it would be if Mr Steele would let him have a go on his tractor. He knew that he *wouldn't*, because it was against the law, but it was nice to dream. He loved mechanical things with the same passion that his sister loved horses.

Fifteen minutes later they turned off the lane into the field next to the Steele's farmhouse. There was no sign of Fiona.

'I'm surprised Fiona isn't out here yet,' said Jane. 'She's so keen on practising her jumping, especially with the gymkhana only two days away.'

Jane dismounted and allowed Misty to crop the grass while she and Charles made their way round to the old outbuildings where Fiona kept her pony, Jupiter. The Steeles didn't have very much money and couldn't afford a smart stable, so Jupiter lived in part of an old barn. It was always kept so spotlessly clean that it wouldn't have disgraced the Royal Mews.

A soft whickering announced the interest of Jupiter. He stuck his glossy black head over the door and nuzzled Jane. He knew that she always kept a packet of Polos in her pocket.

'Hallo, Jupiter,' she said as he crunched happily on a mint. 'What's happened to Fiona?' The pony gave her a rather scornful look, as if he were thinking 'How should I know? No-one tells me anything', and then turned his attention to his haynet at the back of his stall.

Meanwhile, Charles was making a quick

examination of the outhouses. He could find no sign of the new tractor. 'Bother' he thought. 'Mr Steele must be out on it, I suppose.'

Just then Jane and Charles both heard the sound of footsteps approaching, and around the corner of the farmhouse appeared Fiona's father, Mr Steele. With him were P.C. Quipp, the village policeman, and Fiona. Fiona's eyes were pink and her face was rather smudgy. She had obviously been crying.

'Hallo, you're the Patterson children aren't you?' asked P.C. Quipp. 'Have you come round to cheer Fiona up?'

Jane and Charles looked at him blankly. 'I'm sorry, Mr Quipp, but I don't understand what you mean,' said Charles.

'I'm afraid that someone broke into the tackroom during the night and stole Jupiter's new saddle,' Mr Steele explained.

'Goodness! The thieves have struck again,' said Jane. 'How dreadful. Poor old Fiona.'

She looked at Charles. They both knew that Fiona had saved and saved towards the cost of the saddle. She had been getting up at 5.30 on cold, dark winter mornings to do a paper round. She had sold her bike, run errands for the neighbours. She had even washed cars, to pay for half the cost of the saddle. And now it had been stolen.

'Was it insured?' asked Charles, practical as usual.

'Unfortunately not,' said Mr Steele. 'I never got round to it. I'm afraid.'

'Well, sir, we'll do our best to find the saddle for you,' said P.C. Quipp. 'But I can't say that I hold out great hopes. There has been a lot of this type of thieving in the district, and we're pretty sure that the villains move the saddles to other parts of the country to sell them.'

Mr Steele was very angry about the theft but he knew that P.C. Quipp would do his best to catch the thieves.

'Thank you for coming round, Quipp,' he said. 'I'll walk back to your car with you.'

'Goodbye, children,' said P.C. Quipp. 'Don't forget to make sure that your pony's saddle and

tack is kept safely under lock and key.' He and Mr Steele walked off towards the house.

Fiona ran over to Jupiter who came up to the barn door and blew gently down her neck. Jane decided that the best way to cheer Fiona up was to be as cheerful as possible.

'Don't worry. You'll get the saddle back,' she said, though she thought it was rather unlikely.

'Perhaps,' said Fiona, biting her lip and trying hard not to cry. 'But what am I to do? The gymkhana is the day after tomorrow.'

Jane was really sorry for her friend. In fact she felt quite sick with anger. Fiona had a good chance of winning her class. She was a terrific rider and could coax Jupiter over almost anything.

'There must be something we can do!' said Jane. 'I'd lend you Misty's saddle but it would be too small.'

Charles, who had remained very silent, staring into space, as if he hadn't been listening to a word, said:

47

'I know what we can do!'

Jane exchanged glances with Fiona. They both knew that some of Charles' ideas were hopelessly impractical.

'We will set a bait for the robbers and catch them in the act. I bet they won't have got rid of Fiona's saddle yet. They must have to steal quite a few to make it worth their while. So we'll encourage them to steal Misty's.'

'Don't be silly, Charles,' said Jane. 'Mum said that they wouldn't want Misty's saddle. It's rather old, and Jupiter's was brand new.'

'Yes, but they don't know it's old, do they?' muttered Charles, half to himself. Jane and Fiona could almost hear his brain working. He paced up and down the yard with his hands behind this back.

'That's it!' he announced. 'We shall have to start a rumour in the village that Dad has bought Misty a brand new saddle. With any luck the thieves will hear about it and they'll come snooping round to our tackroom – where we shall be waiting for them!'

'Yes, but . . .'

'No buts,' said Charles. 'This is what I want you to do.' As they walked back to the field to collect Misty, he explained his plan to them. All thoughts of the tractor had disappeared from his mind. He was now the great detective – Sherlock Holmes, Hercule Poirot and Magnum all rolled into one. His cool, logical brain, was hot on the trail of the saddle thieves.

'Right, let's go,' he said. 'Fiona and I will walk to the village, to carry out Plan A. You take Misty home, Jane, to prepare for Plan B.'

'I wish I could come with you,' said Jane.

'If one of the villains saw Misty's delapidated old saddle, it would wreck the whole plan, you ninny,' said Charles.

'I suppose so. See you later then,' said Jane. In fact, she was really quite happy to trot Misty home. She much preferred riding to walking!

Charles and Fiona walked into the village which had several shops, two pubs, and a sub-post office.

'Let's try spreading our rumour in the post office first,' said Charles. 'Mrs Smith is the biggest gossip in the village.'

At the post office counter there were several people queueing to collect their pensions, buy stamps and post parcels. To the left, was a counter where a tempting array of chocolates and sweets was on display, as well as an odd assortment of birthday cards, jars of coffee, and packets of soup.

'Hallo, Charlie,' said Mrs Smith. She was so small that she could hardly see over the top of the counter, 'Enjoying the school holidays?'

'Yes, thank you, Mrs Smith,' said Charles politely. He hated people calling him Charlie.

'Where's your sister?' asked Mrs Smith. She liked to know everything that was going on, and

to be the first with any news.

'Oh she's really excited, Mrs Smith. Dad has bought her a super new saddle for Misty. It was ever so expensive and made of the very best leather.'

Fiona felt herself blushing as she heard Charles's fib. Some of the people in the queue turned round to listen.

'What a lucky girl,' said Mrs Smith. 'Well, what can I do for you?'

'This bar of chocolate and some Polos please,' said Charles handing over the exact money.

As he and Fiona walked out he could hear Mrs Smith gossiping about the saddle to her customers. 'It's amazing what parents spend on their children these days. I happen to know that a new saddle costs around £200. Mind you they can afford it. They live in that big house down by the pond, you know.'

Charles and Fiona walked on down the street.

'If I know Mrs Smith,' said Charles 'The news will have travelled across the whole village in about ten minutes. With any luck it will have reached Earlchester by lunchtime!' Earlchester was the neighbouring town, five miles from the village.

'Let's hope that Plan A works and that the crooks really do hear the news,' said Fiona, who was still feeling very downcast.

'Cheer up, Fiona. Look! There's Ted Jennings, the village postman. Let's tell him, too. He's bound to spread the story.'

Postman Ted was about to go into the Pig and Whistle pub for a pint of beer before going home to lunch.

'Hallo, Mr Jennings,' called out Charles. 'Have you finished your post round?'

'Hallo, you two. I delivered two letters for your house today – a gas bill and a letter from your aunt in Australia.' Mr Jennings, like Mrs Smith in the Post Office, was always abreast of the news.

'Guess what, Mr Jennings,' said Fiona. 'Mr Patterson has bought Jane a really expensive new saddle for her pony.'

'Jolly good, jolly good,' said Mr Jennings rather hastily. He was in a hurry to have his pint.

Soon he was sitting comfortably at the bar gossiping with his cronies and spreading the news about Misty's saddle.

'That completes Plan A,' said Charles, as he and Fiona walked back along the village street. 'Now I'd better return home for lunch or I'll be in trouble. I'll ask Mum if you can come for supper and stay the night with Jane and me, so that we can carry out Plan B. We'll say that we would like to sleep in the tent in the garden. They won't suspect anything.'

'Thank you for your help, Charles,' said Fiona shyly. 'See you later then.'

Charles walked home, whistling happily and feeling quite excited about this unexpected adventure.

Over lunch the twins persuaded their mother to have Fiona to stay.

'You won't have to make up a bed for Fiona, Mum,' said Jane. 'It's so warm at the moment that we thought we would put up the tent and camp in the garden.'

'Very well, darling. I'll telephone Mrs Steele, and if she agrees, of course Fiona can come and camp with you.' Mrs Patterson went out to the

hall to make the telephone call. Charles and Jane couldn't hear what she was saying but a few minutes later she returned and said, 'Mrs Steele said that it was an excellent idea. Mr Steele will bring Fiona round at six o'clock.'

'Thank you, Mummy,' Jane said. 'We'd better go and put up the tent.'

So Charles and Jane spent the afternoon preparing for Plan B. First, they put up the tent behind the shrubbery, where it would be hidden from view of the house and the road.

'How did you get on in the tackroom this morning, Jane?' asked Charles, as he fixed the tent poles.

'I gave it a jolly good going over and now it all looks very spick and span. I polished my old swimming cup and put it on display, right in front of the door. It should look very tempting. I only wish I had some riding cups to put there,' said Jane wistfully. 'How did Plan A go?'

'Very well, I think. Fiona and I managed to tell Mrs Smith and Ted Jennings about your brand new saddle. If the thieves are still in the neighbourhood, they're bound to hear the rumour.'

'Fantastic!' said Jane. 'I wish it was time to put Plan B into action. Doesn't time drag by when you are waiting for something exciting to happen.'

During the rest of the day the twins found it dreadfully difficult to keep their plan secret from their parents.

Fiona arrived in time for supper. 'We were very sorry to hear about your saddle, Fiona,' said Mrs Patterson. 'I'm glad to see you looking so cheerful.' Fiona was infected with the twins' sense of excitement and she found it almost impossible not to fidget at the table.

'I must say, Jane,' said Mr Patterson, 'I was very impressed by the state of the tackroom when I inspected it this evening. It looked very tidy. And, by the way, the old padlock looked a bit rusty so I've fitted a large, new one in its place.'

The twins and Fiona stared at each other, wide-eyed, in horrified silence. They had forgotten that Mr Patterson had promised to mend the padlock on the tackroom door. Now that he had fitted a new one the crooks wouldn't be able to get into the tackroom and Plan B would be ruined!

Jane was the first to recover her senses.

'Thank you for fitting a new padlock, Daddy. Um . . . where's the key? I promised Fiona I'd show her Misty's new bridle.'

It's on the shelf in the kitchen. But can't that wait until tomorrow?' said Mr Patterson.

'Oh please, Daddy, please,' begged Jane. Charles and Fiona crossed their fingers behind their backs.

'Very well. But whatever happens, don't lose the key,' said Mr Patterson. 'You can show Fiona the bridle but then it's time for bed.'

'Whew. That was a close run thing,' said Charles after they had said goodnight and gone out to their tent. 'Well done, Jane, for thinking so quickly. Now I'll go and undo the padlock and leave the tackroom door open.' He ran off round the shrubbery towards the tackroom.

'Let's hope that the crooks take the bait and fall into our trap,' said Jane to Fiona. She was not completely convinced that the plan would work. 'Goodness, I hope that I can stay awake,' she added, yawning. They snuggled down in their sleeping bags and when Charles returned to the tent he found them both fast asleep.

'Girls!' snorted Charles. 'They're a fat lot of good,'

In what seemed like only a few minutes – but was, in fact, several hours – Jane felt Charles shaking her.

'Whaaa?' she said sleepily.

'Sssh!' whispered Charles fiercely. 'Luckily I managed to stay awake. A van has just stopped in the road. Come on. It's time to put Plan B into action!

Charles led Jane and Fiona quietly out of the tent and round to the tackroom, where they hid behind the large water-butt, near the open door. Now that Plan B was actually being put into operation he felt rather scared. Supposing it didn't work?

Although it was the middle of the night, they could see quite well because the moon was shining brightly. As they crouched, waiting for the crooks to appear, it seemed to Jane that her heart was thumping so loudly that the thieves were bound to hear it and run away. 'Oh dear. I do hope I don't faint and ruin everything,' she thought. A minute or two later Charles touched her arm. 'Here they come,' he whispered.

Two men appeared from the shrubbery and walked towards the tackroom.

'You're quite sure there are pickings 'ere,

Fred?' said one of them.

'I told yer, didn't I?' replied the shorter of the two men. 'I 'eard it on the grapevine, only today. Look! The door's open. Some people don't 'alf asked to be robbed.'

They tip-toed up to the tackroom door. Behind the water-butt, the three children held hands, almost too frightened to breathe. 'Please go in, please go in,' prayed Fiona.

'Now that's what I called thoughtful. They've left us a bit of silver, too, Sid,' said Fred, who had spotted Jane's swimming cup. 'C'mon, let's be quick about it.'

The two crooks entered the tackroom.

'Right! Come on,' whispered Charles to Jane and Fiona. The three children leapt out from behind the barrels and slammed the tackroom door. Charles shoved the bolt home, and snapped the padlock, his hands shaking with panic.

'Now, Jane, quick. Phone the police,' he gasped. 'Don't just stand there – run!' Jane, who

had been paralysed with fear, turned on her heels and sped like a gazelle to the house.

'Ere, what's going on!' shouted Sid. 'Let us out, we didn't mean no harm.' They banged on the door, and then pressed their faces to the window, trying to catch a glimpse of their captors. Fiona was terrified and clutched Charles.

'It's all right,' said Charles. 'There's no other way out. The window is barred and the door's very strong.'

'Blimey!' said Fred, looking through the window. 'They're only kids.'

'O.K. little 'uns,' Sid shouted in a wheedling manner. 'You've had your fun and it was a good game while it lasted. Now let us out and we can all go 'ome.'

'I'm afraid not,' said Charles sternly. 'The police are on their way.' He hoped they wouldn't be long. It was all very well being a great detective but the truth of the matter was that it was all rather frightening.

To his relief he saw his father dashing towards them waving his torch, with Jane running along behind him.

'Is it really true?' said Mr Patterson. 'Jane's 'phoned the police. She said you'd caught the saddle thieves.'

He heard the banging and crashing from inside the tackroom, accompanied by swearing and threats from Fred and Sid.

'Well, I'll be blowed,' said Mr Patterson. 'They don't sound very happy, do they? You seem to have caught two very angry rats in your trap. You should have told Mummy and me what you were up to, you know. These two could have been very dangerous and you might have been hurt. Still, there's no harm done and I'm proud of you all.

'Now go back to the house, while I wait here for the police. Mummy's boiling up some milk for cocoa.'

The children felt very tired. It was the middle of the night and their adventure had worn them out, but they were still far too excited to go to bed.

The police arrived in two panda cars and the children led them round to the tackroom.

Mr Patterson was still standing guard, but Sid and Fred had given up any hope of getting away. In no time at all the police had snapped handcuffs on the two villains and led them away to the police cars, which were parked by the thieves' van.

Inside the van they found five saddles, including Jupiter's. 'How wonderful!' Fiona cried. 'That's my saddle.'

'I'm afraid we'll need the saddle as evidence at the villains' trial,' said one of the policemen.

'Couldn't you let her have it back temporarily, officer?' asked Mr Patterson. 'She needs it for the gymkhana on Saturday.'

The policeman looked down at Fiona who was biting her lip and trying not to cry.

'Well, as it was these children who caught the robbers, I don't see why not,' he said. 'As long as we can have it back to complete the evidence against the thieves.'

'Oh thank you,' said Fiona. 'And thank you, Charles and Jane. I can't tell you how grateful I am. Thanks to you, tomorrow Jupiter and I can start practising for the gymkhana.'

They all had a wonderful day at the gymkhana. Fiona and Jupiter won their class, and were presented with a red rosette and a cup. Misty was in a mischievous mood and refused at the water, but he won a cup for the best turned-out pony. Jane was thrilled to have a real cup to put in the tackroom with her rosettes. Charles, too, had a wonderful time, looking at the traction engine display and his day was made when he was allowed to climb into the cab of a huge old engine and steer it round the field.

At the end of the day Mrs Smith from the post office came up to the three children.

'If you don't mind my saying so, Jane,' she said patting Misty's neck, 'I think your new saddle looks exactly like the old one.'

She couldn't understand why they all burst out laughing.

'S . . s . . sorry, Mrs Smith,' they gulped. 'It's just that . . . ha . . ha . . ha.'

'Hooorumph,' snorted Misty, joining in the fun, and taking a playful nip at Mrs Smith's hat.

Ten Trusty Tips

Every rider has to start somewhere – but if you don't own a pony you're at a bit of a disadvantage as far as gaining practical experience is concerned! However, with a little determination and dedication there are opportunities for the ponyless to learn and have fun too – helping a friend perhaps, and at Pony Club rallies, of course.

As with other things in life, though, there are a few traps just waiting for the unwary to stumble into – and nothing is worse than learning the hard way. So here are ten trusty tips to help you on your way.

1. Do wear sensible footwear. Once dear old Snowy has carefully placed his foot on top of yours, and has rested his not inconsiderable weight on it, you will soon appreciate the reason why open-toed sandals, trainers or flimsy high heels are not the right gear to wear around the stable yard, however fashionable they may be elsewhere! For stable chores, riding boots or wellies are more sensible. When riding, boots or shoes with a flat sole and small heel are essential, so that your feet do not slide through, or get wedged in the stirrups.

2. Don't stand in front of a pony, for any reason. Even if he is only small, he is still quite a lot heavier and stronger than you are, and it isn't a lot of fun getting trampled on because you were in the way.

3. It doesn't matter which side you lead a pony on, *except on a road.* In this case you should keep yourself between him and the traffic. Watch out for those hooves again. Don't walk in front of him or too close to him, or he will tread all over your heels. When turning, push him away from you, for the same reason. Wear gloves, so that if he pulls, the lead rope won't burn your palms (if he is very strong use a bridle) and *never* wrap it around your hand for better grip. If you do, and he pulls away, you will be unable to let go and will be dragged along behind him – possibly breaking a few bones in your hand at the same time.

4. When tying a pony up, always use a halter or headcollar and lead rope. Never use the reins of the bridle: if he pulls back he may break the

bridle and injure his mouth. Use a quick-release knot, tying the lead rope to a piece of string which will snap in an emergency.

5. Don't grab at a pony's feet when you want to pick them up. If you take him by surprise he may kick out. Let him know where you are first, by talking quietly to him, and then run your hand along his shoulders or quarters and down his legs. Dealing with the hind legs takes a bit of extra care; keep your hand and arm to the inside of the leg, not passing behind it, where it could be injured if he kicks out.

6. The best stable doors have both top and bottom bolts. Make sure that you open the bottom one first, otherwise if the pony inside tries to push out you may receive a hefty bang on the head when you are bending down. Don't forget to close and bolt the door behind you when you go in or out.

7. The only exception to the rule about never standing or walking in front of ponies is when you are leading one through a door or gateway. It should be opened wide. On a windy day prop it open so that it does not blow back as you are halfway through. If you try to squeeze through the gap at the same time, one of you (guess who) will end up getting squashed!

8. All ponies look forward to going out in the field – it is not just an opportunity to eat, but to work off some steam, too. No matter how well behaved your pony is normally, when you are turning him out, always bring him round to face the gate before letting him go. Leave the gate slightly ajar, so that you have room to slip quickly through it if necessary. Remember both of these tips, and you shouldn't find yourself on the receiving end of a hoof if he is excited and has a buck.

9. Most ponies enjoy titbits. Give them on the palm of your hand so that your fingers do not get nipped. *Too many titbits* can make ponies bad tempered, so save such treats for those occasions when he really deserves them. *Praise* is far better for his manners, and is just as well appreciated the rest of the time. If you do want to give him a pat, make sure that it is on his neck or shoulder. Giving his face a vigorous pat or his quarters a hearty slap will only frighten or startle him.

10. The last golden rule to remember is easy. Be observant and sensitive to a pony's needs and moods – and always use your common sense!

Views from Bridle Paths

2. In the Country

The countryside has a variety of habitats. Some of them are contained in natural features of the landscape. Others have been shaped by the use of land for agriculture.

As most bridle paths follow hedgerows or field margins, a wealth of wildlife can be discovered. On a typical ride you will see:

Birds. Many of them feed, find shelter, and nest in the hedgerows. Trees. Hedge climbers with colourful flowers and autumn fruits. Wild flowers. Butterflies. Crops. Rabbits and, more rarely, hares.

KESTREL

CHAFFINCH + NEST

SWALLOW (summer)

GOLDFINCH

YELLOWHAMMER

DUNNOCK (Hedge sparrow) + NEST

JAY

ROOK

BULLFINCH

CROW

REDWING (winter)

PHEASANT

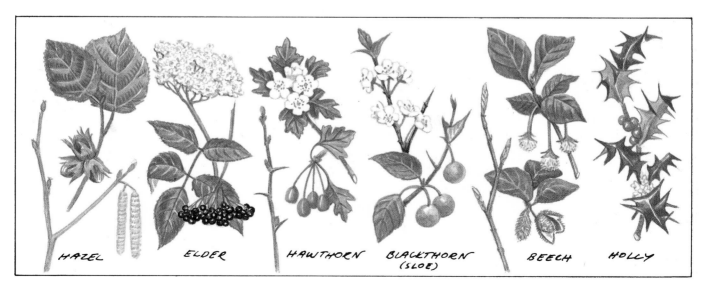

HAZEL   ELDER   HAWTHORN   BLACKTHORN (SLOE)   BEECH   HOLLY

DOG ROSE BRAMBLE BINDWEED HONEYSUCKLE BLACK BRYONY TRAVELLER'S JOY

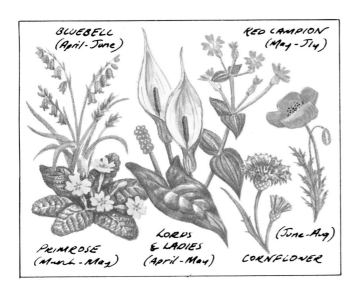

BLUEBELL (April-June)   RED CAMPION (May-Jly)

PRIMROSE (March-May)   LORDS & LADIES (April-May)   CORNFLOWER (June-Aug)

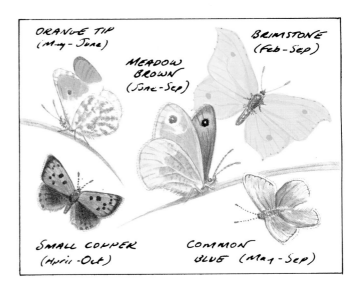

ORANGE TIP (May-June)   MEADOW BROWN (June-Sep)   BRIMSTONE (Feb-Sep)

SMALL COPPER (April-Oct)   COMMON BLUE (May-Sep)

WHEAT   OATS   BARLEY   RYE   OILSEED RAPE

RABBIT

BROWN HARE

The Warrior Breed

Sylvia Loch

Can you imagine the feeling inside you – if you had never in your life seen a horse, never seen a picture of one, never read a book, never enjoyed television, never even been told about horses or indeed understood that such an animal existed – if suddenly you were confronted by a crowd of armed men on horseback? Imagine it! You look again, disbelieving at first. But it is all real. Wet from the sea from whence they have come, they gallop towards you – etched darkly against the white sand, menacing and bold. Can you imagine how you would feel?

The year is 1519 AD and as the sun gleams on the invading Spaniards' breastplates and bounces off their cutlasses and swords, the horses plunge beneath them, curvetting and rearing in the way they have been taught for battle. The air fills with neighing, snorting, the jangling of curb and armour and the shouting and screaming of the riders. It is an awesome spectacle for the peace-loving Mexican Indians emerging from their jungle cover to greet these strangers from the sea. We can scarcely conceive the wonder, the fear – for some the sudden horror – of this vision.

Some Indians are trembling, bewildered, perplexed. They think it must be their serpent god, Quetzalcoatl, come in vengeance in a different centaur-like form. What have they done to deserve this fearful apparition? Wait. The beasts move as one . . . or do they? There are two heads – is it two separate beings? It is all a nightmare . . . mark the white foam that erupts from one set of mouths? Will they spit fire too – perhaps to devour them all? Or will they simply strike them down with those flailing iron-clad feet? The Indians cower back, now desperately afraid.

This may sound remote and fanciful but it did actually happen – less than five hundred years ago. Cortés was the great Spanish leader who landed his horses and men on the Mexican mainland to claim the continent for God and King. For two years he and his horsemen marched and fought their way through the wild, mountainous and treacherous countryside until at last they wrested the capital, Tenochtitlan

This statue is a fine replica of the Iberian or Spanish horse as used by the Conquistadores in the sixteenth century. Note the powerful neck and shoulder, the 'Roman' head, and the ease with which the stallion raises his front legs.

(now Mexico City), from the Aztecs. With fewer than a hundred horsemen in the final assault, the Spaniards outwitted and overcame literally thousands of Indians; it could have been a miracle. Thus was established the importance and superiority of the horse for ever in the New Country. Mainly because of the horse, the Iberian empire then spanned the world, from the Philippines to Panama, bringing untold wealth to the Spanish and Portuguese crowns.

Until that invasion, the Americas had been without the horse since prehistoric times. Its peoples, mainly Aztecs and Inca Indians, were totally ignorant of its existence. This is perhaps hard to imagine for us today. America is now so full of horses, both in the South, the Central zone and in the Northern territories of the United States and Canada, we take them for granted. We have all heard of the famous Quarter Horse, favourite of the cowboys; the pintos and paints prized by the Indians; the famous mustangs of the prairies; the pacers, amblers and trotters, as well as popular breeds such as the Morgan, but how many of us realise that many of these breeds simply would not exist in their present form if it had not been for the Conquistadores and their horses?

The Spanish shipped with them proud Iberian stallions and mares, famed throughout Europe as the mounts of kings, and the forefathers of so many famous breeds today – the Andalusian, the Lusitano, and the Lipizzaner, to name the most direct. These horses had been used in battle since long before even the time of the Romans. They were older by far than the Arab horse of the desert, and were prized by the ancient Greeks and the Spartans. They were reputed to have spread even as far afield as China. Their origins dated back to prehistoric times when cave

The Spanish and Portuguese have been transporting their warhorses by sea for centuries before the Conquest of the Americas. However, to endure the crossing of the Atlantic Ocean, the horse had to survive extremes of discomfort, weather and conditions. The engraving on the right, from *Manejo Real (Madrid, 1769)*, shows how they were slung on to the outer deck.

The illustration below of a typically Spanish or Portuguese saddle horse displays the main characteristics to look out for in the American and other breeds descended from him. Note in particular the shape of the head, so different from the dished profile of the Arab.

A deeply set, powerful, rather upright neck often with a slightly wavy mane

A short back, fairly wide loins, sloping croup and low-set tail

Convex profile 'Roman-nosed'

Powerful padded chest and shoulder

High-stepping with rounded knee action

Neat, round, rather high hooves

Powerful hocks stepping well under the body

During the sixteenth and seventeenth centuries all the kings of Europe were mounted on Spanish horses. This was the golden age of chivalry and of daring, and you were no one if you were not enthroned on a warhorse from the Iberian Peninsula. Here we see Emperor Charles V (Charles I of Spain), under whose patronage Cortés invaded the New World, mounted on a Spanish charger.

paintings found in southern Spain depicted a proud, up-headed animal with a strong neck, short body and ram-shaped face. Later this came to be called 'Roman-nosed', since the shape resembled the noticeably powerful features of the Roman nobility.

The word Conquistadore means Conqueror – Lord of the Conquest. In the fifteenth and sixteenth centuries, Spain and Portugal, which jointly make up the Iberian Peninsular, boasted a huge expanding empire. If you have not heard of Cortés who conquered Mexico, you will certainly have heard of the Spanish explorer Christopher Columbus, who first discovered America. You may also know about the Portuguese Ferdinand Magellan, the first man to sail round the world.

These early explorers were not only inspired by love of their country and their religion. They were also filled with the spirit of adventure. This was the age of chivalry and of daring, and to fulfil the role of cavalier you had to have a good horse. Everyone wanted an Iberian charger; in the same way that people today like an expensive make of car. In the sixteenth and seventeenth centuries you were nobody unless you owned a Spanish or Portuguese horse. In fact all the heads of Europe were mounted on Iberian horses, including Queen Elizabeth I, King James I and King Charles I. There are many famous pictures of Charles I mounted on a Spanish charger by the court painter, Van Dyck; the most famous of them hangs in London's National Gallery, but there are others all over Britain, including Warwick Castle and Buckingham Palace.

Why was the Spanish horse so special? Why did everybody want one, and what attributes fitted this horse for battle in a way no other horse could equal?

Firstly, the Iberian horses were extremely hardy. Although they were the aristocrats of the horse world in those days (long before the Arab had come to Europe or the Thoroughbred had evolved) they were economical to keep, tolerating quite basic conditions. They were sound of heart and limb. And they could travel all day and all night non-stop if necessary.

Secondly, they were willing. Possessing a remarkably sweet temperament, they were easy to school and to train for battle. Dog-like in their devotion, they became very attached to one master and took a delight in their training, however arduous. This could mean the difference between life and death for the rider. With a horse that was easily taught, and who understood all

A modern Spanish horse ridden by a rider from the Andalusian School of Equestrian Art. So little has changed since the time of Cortés. The horses still display the courage, agility and obedience which made them so popular in the sixteenth and seventeenth centuries. Still today they practise the beautiful battle manoeuvres for which they were famed.

the intricate battle manoeuvres, you stood a fair chance of surviving a mounted duel with pistol or sword. On a stubborn, less schooled horse, the risk was very great.

Thirdly, the Iberian horses were brave. By the sixteenth century, tales of their courage had reached England, and chroniclers, including the Duke of Newcastle, tell heart-rending stories of how these brave stallions continued to perform for their masters until the bitter end – even after they had been fatally wounded.

The Conquistadores themselves very much appreciated their horses. One of the writers on the Cortés expedition wrote: 'Horses are the most necessary thing in the New Country because they frighten the enemy most, and after God, to them belongs the victory.'

We know indeed that Cortés cared deeply about every one of his horses. His own black stallion, Mortzillo, campaigned with him all the way from Mexico to Guatemala, and he was broken-hearted when he had to leave him behind in the care of some Indians because of a poisoned hoof. In his long letters to Spain, telling his King and Emperor, Charles V, about his victories for the Spanish Crown, Cortés always included tales of the horses. When a mare was wounded at the capture of Mexico City he and his men 'grieved exceedingly'. In the heat of victory, there was still genuine caring.

The time was coming when the Indians would themselves find a way of acquiring horses. Once they had overcome their initial fear, they raided the Spanish studs, and either captured the horses that they wanted, or released them into the wild. Soon foals were born in Indian encampments or survived far out in the jungle or prairie without the help of man.

A lot can happen in a hundred years in the animal kingdom. By 1650, the Apaches, one of the most warlike Indian tribes, were all mounted. There were horses everywhere. Many Indians did not even bother to breed them. When they wanted a horse, they simply rode out into the wild and captured one. Other tribes followed suit, and from there on the stories of the Wild West, which we all know so well, began. One cannot blame people for forgetting that the horse in America began with the Spaniards and not with the Indians.

Many of today's American breeds reflect the old Spanish characteristics. Most modern mustangs are smaller than the original Spanish horses; this is because they have had to fend for themselves, often in difficult conditions, for many centuries. The Indians always took the biggest and best for riding, so only the poorer specimens were left to breed. But where the mustang has been domesticated, we are seeing a return to a strong and stocky horse, and the old Spanish colours of grey, roan, dun and bay are prevalent, often with a dorsal stripe. Many of the pintos, paints and Appaloosas still have a Spanish look about them. People say they are all descended from two coloured horses on Cortés' expedition, Moron and Baena. Think of coloured or spotted horses you know, and see if they have Spanish characteristics. We have already described the Iberian horse's temperament. Physical features to spot are:

- A distinctive convex profile (see illustration) – sometimes called 'Roman-nosed'.

- A deeply set, powerful and rather upright neck often with a slightly wavy mane.

- High stepping, with rounded knee action and strong powerful hocks which move well underneath the body.

- A short back, fairly wide at the loins and a somewhat low-set tail (unlike the Arab).

- Neat, round, rather high hooves.

These are the Iberian characteristics. As well as having all-round performance and a super nature, horses with this genetic background are usually very comfortable to ride, making them popular saddle horses, just like their ancestors.

If you really want to see for yourself the kind of horse that Cortés rode, you can do no better than go to Spain or Portugal and seek out the national studs. But there are now many purebred Andalusians and Lusitanos all over the world, and through their respective breed societies you will find fine examples.

The horse of kings – the horse of the conquest – really does still exist. He is the oldest saddle horse in the world and not only has he left his mark on all the horses of the Americas, but also on many European breeds. You will find him in art galleries and cast in bronze as grand statues in our parks and squares. He is the horse of history, and he is all around us if we will only look for him.

Characters

IN ...

NICOLA NOVELLO
VALERIE WHITE
CYRIL WHEELER
PAMELA COVENEY
JOYCE CAREY
PERLITA NEILSON
DOROTHY BATLEY
CONSTANCE LORNE

magic there is in

PROGRA

OPENING APPEAL BY   Susan Stranks

INTRODUCTION MARCH   THE HAMPSHIRE SCHOOL.

DRILL   JUNIOR PUPILS

POEM—HIEDEROSLEIN   SENIOR PUPILS

A BALLROOM LESSON

ASSISTANTS: Rosemary Allen, Linda Bathurst, Patricia Beckwith, Jane Beyfus, Gylda Bunday, Primrose Coulter, Clare Coulter, Carole Dowell, Susan Hampshire, Gail Horsfall, Elizabeth Larcher, Helen Noble, Ann Pearce, Elizabeth Saunders, Susan Stranks.

PUPILS: Christopher Allen, Brian Carroll, Richard Curvalho, David Collis, Anthony Dowell, Anthony Elliott, Nicholas French, Anthony Kelson, Tom La Dell, Rupert Lowder, Timothy Maltby, Nicholas Merrimen, Charl Richards, Jason Wilson, Norman Wilson.

JUNIOR BALLROOM PUPILS: Dorothy Anderson, Catherine Ash, Vivian Ashton, Georgina Barker, Celia Carroll, Daphne Carroll, Victoria Clinkard, Sandra Doxart, Sherry D'oyly, Veronica Elliott, Angela Fitch, Maina Gielgud, Annette Garrick, Luella Garrick, Julia Higgs, Gillian McIver, Penelope Masser, Melanie Mackenzie, Jennifer Neave, Diana Nowton, Virginia Orr, Gail Orr, Alison Skemp, Kathy Trent, Sarah Wolpe, Debroah Wolpe.

POETRY   KINDERGARTEN PUPILS

DASHING AWAY WITH THE SMOOTHING IRON   JUNIOR PUPIL

A Vision Achieved

The founder and her daughters – Mrs June Hampshire with Jane and Ann.

A Vision Achieved

A HISTORY OF THE HAMPSHIRE SCHOOLS

1928 – 1995

DAVID LEMMON

The Hampshire School 50th Anniversary
Educational Trust

Published by The Hampshire School 50th Anniversary Educational Trust
Registered Charity Number 280556

© 1996 The Hampshire School 50th Anniversary Educational Trust

A CIP catalogue record for this book is available from the British Library.

ISBN 0 9527527 0 0

Designed by Jim Reader
Jacket designed by Peter Dolton

Production in association with Book Production Consultants plc,
25–27 High Street, Chesterton, Cambridge CB4 1ND, UK

Typeset by Cambridge Photosetting Services
Printed and bound in Singapore by Kyodo Printing Co (S'pore) Pte Ltd

The Hampshire School logo was designed/drawn by Donald Pavey, derived from the
Pavey family crest
The illustrations on the endpapers were kindly provided from the archives of The
Hampshire Schools

Contents

Acknowledgements

his history has been compiled by David Lemmon – a well-known professional author, biographer and editor with more than thirty books published in the United Kingdom. He was in the teaching profession for many years before turning to authorship as a full-time occupation.

His connection with The Hampshire Schools stems from his long friendship with Jane and Christopher Box-Grainger. In his capacity as editor of *The British Theatre Yearbook*, he was the adjudicator of the School's annual play competition in 1984. He visited the three School buildings during 1995 but his major task has been the examination of very many School papers and registers, magazines and former pupils' bulletins, press cuttings, programmes and photographs. The Trustees of The Hampshire School 50th Anniversary Education Trust are most grateful for his outstanding contribution to this book.

The Trustees also acknowledge with gratitude permission to reproduce portraits painted by Mrs Catherine Davies and the late David Kemp, ARA, and the many photographs provided by Alexandra Studios, Ashdown Press, John Douglas, Colin Maher and Guy Rivière.

Some pages are enlivened with drawings by past and present pupils of The Hampshire School, who also contributed ideas for the illuminated capital letters at the start of each chapter.

Finally, the hours of proof-reading and correction of text and captions by individual Trustees must also be recorded with equal gratitude.

Foreword

I am delighted and honoured to be asked to write this foreword to a book which celebrates the history of a truly remarkable school and, in particular, the accomplishment of an even more remarkable and talented woman.

Mrs June Hampshire had a great influence on my early life at school, instilling in me a love of the theatre and dancing which was to shape my future. But while normal education at The Hampshire School was a subtle mixture of learning and fun, Mrs Hampshire and her two daughters, Ann and Jane, trained us all in self-discipline. 'The show had to go on' no matter what we were doing – conventional examinations, appearances on many stages in aid of charities, even the clearing of tables for lessons and lunch!

Looking back, I think that the most significant lesson I learned from my time at the little school in St Saviour's Hall, was the importance of discipline – the discipline to drive mind and body forward to higher goals and achievement. The Hampshire School taught one that no pinnacle of success in any sphere of life was unattainable – difficulties and problems were there simply to be overcome.

I do wish this charming and unusual history, and the Trust which has had the courage to produce it, every possible success. I very much hope that the children of today's Hampshire Schools will take heart and inspiration from the wisdom and experience gathered in these pages, and I wish them well in all their endeavours.

Sir Anthony Dowell, CBE
Director, The Royal Ballet

CAPITOL CAFÉ RESTAURANT
Open daily 11 a.m. till 1 p.m.

SPECIAL INCLUSIVE LUNCHEON & CINEMA
3 COURSES AND A SEAT IN CINEMA

2/-

OUR TASTEFULLY DECORATED BALLROOM
(WITH LATEST HOLOPHANE LIGHTING) MAY BE HIRED.

The Jane Ann School of Dancing, Music and Elocution was first started by Jane Ann with the intention of trying to help others to enjoy the Arts she loves most. Now the school has grown very large, with its main training studio in Sloane Street, Knightsbridge, and branches in Cheam, Epsom, Banstead, Sutton and Hampstead.

The small children taking lessons only learn steps which are beneficial to their bodies, as Jane Ann herself, being the mother of three children, is strongly against OVER-TRAINING little ones.

Classes for these are held separately, and already several are taking up dancing as a profession at the school. Many girls at the age of sixteen and seventeen are taking up dancing as a profession at the school.

Mr. Anton Dolin, our greatest dancer, who opened the London School, has, this month, chosen pupils to dance in the ballet of his next film, in which he will be appearing with Miss Lillian Harvey.

For particulars of classes please write to JANE ANN,
THE CAPITOL, EPSOM,
CHEAM HALL, CHEAM,
OAKGATE, CUDDINGTON AVENUE, EWELL,
Telephone : Ewell 1625,
or
2, BASIL STREET, SLOANE STREET, S.W.3,
Telephone : Kensington 4193.

JANE ANN wishes to thank all parents and children, and the following
co-operation in the production—

THE MANAGEMENT OF THE CAPITOL

THE COMMITTEE OF THE CHILDREN'S WARD OF THE EPSOM COTTAGE

MISS MOLLY GODDARD   MISS OLGA WEBB

MISS KATHLEEN MUNN, A.R.C.M.   MISS PEGGY RENTO

MY STAFF AND STUDENTS

and particularly

THE ADVERTISERS—**PLEASE** give them your support.

Costumes in Part II, No. 2, are from Mr. Anton Dolin's late B

Next production by Jane Ann :—Dances in 'The Hangman,' at the Arts

Programme for a recital
at the Capitol, Epsom.

THE importance of dancing as a "vital form of bodily exercise" is emphasised by Sir George Newman in his annual report, as Chief Medical Officer of the Board of Education, on "The Health of the School Child." He speaks of it as "a valuable means of educating body, mind and character in one harmonious whole." Dr. Norwood, and Sir Michael Sadler, at the recent Public Health Congress, have had some hard things to say about the one-sidedness of our system of education, the lack of real physical training, of education in the arts. Dancing not only trains the muscles of the body, develops the sense of balance and movement. It is an art, and, moreover, natural to children as an expression of happiness.

Jane & Ann in costume

*"Do not grow old"
is the motto
of a dancer*

Dancing is an Art for which we, both young and old, should be grateful, for it is never too late to carry out beautiful movements to music. Some great ballroom dancers have not indeed had lessons or danced until they were over fifty.

the Hampshire philosophy!

Firm Foundations

une Hampshire was born to dance and teach. She believed that dancing was an art for which young and old should ever be grateful. This history will reveal the vision of the founder and her daughters, and how they created the schools now known as The Hampshire Schools.

However, the story would not be complete without recognition of the contributions of generations of parents, staff and pupils. Also one cannot exclude the great support of the world of dance, the Former Pupils' Association, the Parents' Association and the Trustees of the 50th Anniversary Educational Trust – all remembered in this history.

To begin the story, it is necessary to touch on the personal life of June Hampshire which, as you will read, did so much to influence the development of the School. Her husband, George Kenneth Hampshire, from whom the School derived its name, was a handsome and clever man. As a boy he had won a scholarship to Leeds Grammar School and, later, an exhibition to Magdalen College, Oxford – where he read science and left with a double first. His energies were not restricted exclusively to academic life, for he was a keen oarsman. He rowed at number five in the Magdalen College eight which won the Head of the River Race in 1923, and in the number three position in the Magdalen four which won the Visitors' Cup at Henley in the same year.

On leaving Oxford, he joined the firm of Brunner Mond as a research chemist. In the summer of 1923, at a party in London, he met June Pavey, who became his wife on 9 May 1924.

June Hampshire, under her stage name of June Pavois, had danced with the D'Oyly Carte Opera Company and had also enjoyed considerable success in a production of Graham Moffat's Scottish comedy *Bunty Pulls the Strings*. Like her husband, she was the youngest of a large family. Her father, Arthur Pavey, was a solicitor and her mother Jane (née Petley) had served as a volunteer nurse during the Great War. Most of Jane Pavey's life, however, was spent tied to her Wimbledon home rearing her six children – five boys and her one daughter, June.

In a house dominated by men, June's mother was protective of her only daughter, and even kept her from attending school on the slightest pretext. So, dance was to become June's passion and means of escape from the confines of home. But later, she was to recognise the benefits of education at home. Life was to present her with many challenges, and she was able to meet them boldly and bravely and to remain unbowed and unbeaten.

June Hampshire possessed personal magnetism, and most people fell under her spell. Olga Webb, a former pupil, wrote: 'My first glimpse of this enchanting woman fascinated me. With her copper auburn hair, elfin face and figure, she radiated vitality. Her dancing brown eyes showed such a sense of the joy of living.' So it is not difficult to understand the attraction she had for Kenneth Hampshire. She was intelligent and possessed of the same dynamism by which he himself was driven.

June's childhood had not been an easy one, but her marriage was to pose problems of a different nature. Kenneth was very devoted to his work and he was ambitious. He rose to become chairman of the General Chemicals Division of ICI and a main board director of that renowned company. He was a remarkable man, destined to achieve success.

The problem was that June was a remarkable woman who was also destined to achieve. She saw no joy in the life to which her mother had been subjected, and she rejected the role of subservient housewife. She had a passion for work, she had tasted success in the theatre and she could claim as friends many of the leading artistic figures of the time. She was, perhaps, something of an anachronism – an emancipated woman who refused to be a second-class citizen. Events were to aid her liberation.

The Hampshire home was in Surrey, at Oakgates, but Kenneth's work

Oakgates in Surrey, the Hampshire family home.

was to take him to the North, and he was to travel widely. The Hampshire marriage became a passage of long separations, yet this fragmented relationship was to produce four highly talented children. The first was Jane, who will play a leading rôle in this story. The second was Ann, a gifted teacher of young children who was also a good pianist and was to become a much-loved teacher of the piano. The third child was John, now a successful hotelier in Austria. Lastly came Susan – destined to be a very successful actress and author. Sparked by the energy of their mother, the four children were to become a family of many and diverse talents.

June Hampshire's vision of the future began to take shape. In 1928, she founded The Jane Ann School of Dancing in Surrey by holding classes in the drawing-room of her handsome house, while taking the professional name of Jane Ann.

It came as no surprise that the new school was an immediate success. June had too much vitality and expertise for it to be anything else. She drove people forward with joy and vigour, and they responded to her motto – 'Dancers Do Not Grow Old!'

The School soon outgrew the drawing-room at Oakgates, making it necessary to rent the local Cheam Hall and then various other halls in

'Tarantella' Group at
Cheam Hall.

Surrey. More space was obtained in 1933 by renting the ballroom of the
Drift Bridge Hotel at Epsom. Two years later, a lease was taken out on an
attractive studio in Epsom High Street. Full-time training was provided
for students of ballet, ballroom-dancing, tap-dancing and musical comedy.
There were students of all ages who accepted June's dancer's motto!

In spite of these developments in Surrey, the most significant venture
in the years before the Second World War was the opening of June's
London Ballet School, following the birth of her third child, John. She
took a lease on the mezzanine floor of No. 2 Basil Street, Knightsbridge
– almost parallel to Brompton Road from Sloane Street and immediately behind Harrods. The new school was welcomed warmly and opened
with a champagne reception, the guests including leading figures in the
world of ballet and influential members of the press. One of the most
ardent supporters of June's new school was the great dancer, Anton Dolin.

Allied to her excellence as a teacher, June had an urgent and far-
seeing quality which recognised the necessity of broadening the courses

'The Jane Ann Follies' of 1934 – (left to right) Phyllis Stoneham, Pat Marchant, Elizabeth Gorman, Audrey Anthill and Jean Park.

she offered. By 1935, advertising in *The Dancing Times*, The Jane Ann School of Dancing and The London Ballet School could point to classes in Sutton, Cheam, Epsom, Staines, Limpsfield and even Letchworth – with additional tuition in elocution, music and dramatic art. The London Ballet School in Basil Street was able to offer shorthand, typing and French for seniors; and professional training for the stage. In that same year, June claimed that stage and film experience could be provided for those professional students during such training. This claim was substantiated by the fact that some of her students had appeared in two popular and successful films – *Lorna Doone*, starring Margaret Lockwood and John Loder, and *Autumn Crocus*, starring Ivor Novello and Fay Compton. Both films were directed by Basil Dean.

Among the children to appear in the films were Jane and Ann Hampshire. Often as a duet, the sisters made regular appearances in concerts and recitals given by the Jane Ann School to help raise money for worthy causes, mainly based in Surrey – but there were no geographical restrictions on June Hampshire's students: they appeared in a major theatrical garden party in the Royal Botanical Gardens, Regent's Park, in aid of the Actors' Orphanage at Langley Hall. Noël Coward presided over the occasion, and Jane and Ann were part of *Euphan Maclaren's Cabaret Tea* in the 'Gaumont Palace'. Nigel Stock, Wendy Toye and Betty Bucknall were among the celebrities with whom they appeared.

Later, the Hampshire sisters were to be seen at the Capitol Theatre, Epsom, where the Jane Ann School gave a concert to help fund a children's ward for the local cottage hospital. Young John Hampshire also appeared in this concert – much later, in 1948 he played a part in the film *The Guinea Pig*, starring Richard Attenborough.

June Hampshire's view of education was, for her time, broad and visionary. As we know, she numbered among her friends leading dancers such as Anton Dolin – but also painters, poets and artistic figures of the stature of Edith Sitwell. June wanted her charges to be exposed to the fullest possible range of cultural activities; always concerned within the conventions of society to develop full, rounded and articulate human beings. But, during the mid-1930s, June was unable to provide a full educational programme; nor did she consider undertaking the complete education of her own children at that time. The classes in Knightsbridge and Surrey thrived, but the political situation in Europe grew worse month by month. What some remember as the 'long, halcyon summer', and what W. H. Auden described as the 'dishonest decade', was coming to a close. In September 1939 came the outbreak of the Second World War, and the Hampshire children were evacuated from London to North Wales in 1940. June's teaching activities in London and Surrey came to an end. Jane and Ann, relocated to Pengwern Hall in North Wales, were immersed in a new and very different environment – although Jane found herself to be in luck, for she came under the influence of another remarkable teacher of dance, Dorothy Aburrow.

June Hampshire's energies were diverted into a different direction. She enlisted in the Women's Auxiliary Air Force (WAAF) and travelled far and wide, finding herself for a period at the RAF Fighter Station at Wick in the far north of Scotland. During 1943, one of the first flying bombs fell next to the Hampshire home at Oakgates. The house was severely damaged, and never again could it be used for the teaching of dancing. In reality, the first phase in the history of The Hampshire School was at an end.

During her absence in the WAAF, June allowed her Basil Street studio to be used by such renowned teachers of ballet as Vera Volkova and Flora Fairbain – they defied bombs and 'doodle-bugs' to give private lessons to advanced pupils who were likely to become stars in the theatre of the future.

June's service in the WAAF came to an end in 1944 and, later that year, she returned to London to resume occupancy of the studio in Basil Street. It was not simply that she was restless and eager to resurrect her career as a teacher. She was now beset by a personal worry – namely, the education of her fourth child, Susan. Throughout her life, June had confronted all problems with courage and determination that sprang from the resources within herself. She was concerned about the education of a young daughter, but the solution to the problem was simple. She would educate that daughter herself! Once that decision had been taken, there remained the challenges of finance and organisation. Again, her response was forthright. An advertisement appeared in the Personal column of *The Times*:

'Mrs G. K. Hampshire is looking for some children to share first school lessons with her daughter, Susan, in Knightsbridge...'

The reaction to the advertisement was as immediate as it was warm. The first pupils to join Susan were Sandra Mason, Michael Pocock, Sarah Searight and Rosemary Watson. Incidentally, Rosemary is now Mrs Rosemary Ashby, President of Pine Manor College in Massachusetts, USA. She is also a member of the Board of The Hampshire School 50th Anniversary Educational Trust and a distinguished academic. She has written:

'I believe I was among the very first students of The Hampshire School at its Basil Street site following the introduction of the academic curriculum. I was more or less a contemporary of Susan Hampshire and my teachers were Miss Jane and Miss Ann. I see them both with hair pulled severely back in ballerina style, gliding about. Of course we all wanted to be like them, and what a sad disappointment it was to discover one wasn't destined to be another Beryl Grey! My most vivid recollections are of dancing to the music of a piano in a large studio, picknicking in Hyde Park and reading voraciously at a very young age. I remember being taken upstairs to watch a cooking demonstration. I fretted about having to sit still and observe, and was excused. When the mouth-watering product materialized, I was not allowed a taste because I had opted out of the process. Discipline was constructive and instructive at The Hampshire School! Looking back, I think I brought away from the School a great love of music, dance, movement and the outdoors – a lifelong habit of reading, learning, love of adventure and enthusiasm for life. June Hampshire's legacy surely.'

Mrs June Hampshire.

Mrs Hampshire's School, as it was then known, had come into being and was an instant success. Its reputation grew rapidly, and more and more parents sought places for their young children.

The acquisition of larger premises became a priority. In 1946 St Saviour's Hall in Walton Place was rented – Basil Street continues past Harrods into Walton Place, so the move of some 300 yards was easy.

Of the studio in Basil Street, Olga Webb wrote nostalgically:

'It was quite perfect with a beautiful sprung maple floor and mirrors of different sizes and shapes, so that dancers could see themselves in action from any part of the Studio. I remember especially the decor in green and white, and the frilly net curtains fluttering in the breeze – but pride of the whole place was the white Bechstein baby grand piano.'

However, one must consider that, by the strict school building standards of today, both the Basil Street Studio and St Saviour's Hall failed

St Saviour's Hall before improvement – Ann Hampshire with junior pupils, including Charles Batty, Caroline Bayliss, Simon de Wardener, Gail Horsfall, Ann Gary Lee, Alan Maltby, Amanda Trench.

to offer ideal facilities in which to house schools. A former pupil described the Hall: 'We entered through a small dark Vestry, where we used to hang our coats. There was a small cloakroom adjoining the Vestry which we hardly ever used. We went into the Hall through swing doors, where there was plenty of room to run and play. At the far end, there were two more cloakrooms – one for girls and one for boys.' The Hall provided a single large area in which children learnt, ate and played under close supervision.

This description hardly suggests a recipe for resounding success, but the School indeed became so, and a year later it was registered formally as The Hampshire School – and the story proper begins.

It should be recalled that this was a time of hope. In spite of 'austerity', the rebuilding and restructuring of Britain and its institutions after the ravages of the war did generate a mood of optimism wherein all things seemed possible. June Hampshire had ever been in tune with such a mood. She would never have survived had she not been perpetually optimistic and energetic; driven by the desire to work.

The astonishing success of the School was unquestionable. June was a brilliant teacher of dance, and enlightened educationalist and dedicated to the development and welfare of her pupils. But, like many others gifted with rare artistic ability, she lacked business acumen. There were times

An outing to Chessington Zoo in 1949. The group includes Christopher Allen, Tess Ashton, Charles Batty, Caroline Bayliss, Patricia Beckwith, Jennifer Bembridge, Jane Beyfus, Sandra Mary Cheatle, Simon de Wardener, Frances Donaldson, Anthony Dowell, Carole Dowell, Anthony Elliott, Anne Foulsham, Alexander Guthrie, Susan Hampshire, Benjamin Hoare, Richard Hoare, Nicholas Jack, Sally Kidd, Susan Leon, Rosemary Lord, Alan Maltby, Sandra Mason, Gillian McIver, Sheila Moseley, Juliet Musker, Patrick Nangle, Simone Nangle, Jennifer Neave, Simon Neave, Helen Noble, Patrick Orr, Griselda Pocock, Anne Searight, Julia Snow, Sarah Steiner, Elwyn Stock, Susan Stranks, Amanda Trench, Jonathan Trench, Catherine Turner, Christopher Turner, Sarah Wolpe.

when this lack was to prove most costly. The parents included a number of well-known artists and illustrators, and she would accept their works of art in lieu of school fees. Rather sadly, she missed opportunities to expand the potential of the School by leasing more suitable premises. Perhaps this was a deliberate policy on June's part for, in her heart, she wanted nothing to threaten the warm and cosy atmosphere of the 'little school in the Hall'. What mattered to her most was the ethos of that special environment, and we should consider how quickly that remarkable and magical ethos was achieved.

There were limitations at St Saviour's Hall but these were balanced by considerable advantages. The Hall was situated in a fashionable part of London, and many of the parents were prestigious and influential people. They were loyal to the School, its aims and objectives – they 'spread the word' – and no school can wish for a better asset than this.

The Hall was rented on an hourly basis, and costs were low. In comparison with the salaries and allowances paid in later years, the salaries of the teaching staff were also low – accordingly, school fees were not expensive. However, undeterred by the poor remuneration, the teaching was fresh and inspiring. June had asked her two elder daughters, Jane

Summer in Hyde Park, 1950 – Miss Jane with pupils, including Janet Batchelor, Linda Bathurst, Caroline Bayliss, Patricia Beckwith, Jennifer Bembridge, Sandra Mary Cheatle, Frances Donaldson, Carole Dowell, Oliver Gildersleeve, Susan Hampshire, Selina Ling, Juliet Musker, Patrick Nangle, Simone Nangle, Anne Searight, Susan Stranks, Christopher Turner.

and Ann, to join her at the School and they helped to form the nucleus of a small but dedicated team. It was obvious that there would be confusion if both daughters were referred to as 'Miss Hampshire', so June decided that they should be known as Miss Jane and Miss Ann. This mode of address was extended to almost all other members of staff, and it came to reflect the special nature and attraction of the School. This was a family; this was like a home; here was warmth.

Carole Stephen-Lane (née Carole Dowell, Sir Anthony Dowell's sister) writes:

'It was a unique school, incorporating formal education within the School and experience of the outside world. We performed concerts in real theatres and I remember we also had an English lesson on *Silas Marner*, reading aloud in a cosy Knightsbridge coffee shop. In passing, we learnt table manners, how to order from the menu and even how to pay the bill! We visited art galleries, museums, theatres and parks. We went to the Old Vic to be enriched by the plays of Shakespeare. This very broad education gave me self-confidence, and the inner strength for the life I was to lead in the theatre and all over the world.'

Members of staff outside St Saviour's Hall in 1953 – Mrs Betty Peck, Miss Shirley Knowles, Miss Freda Green, Mrs June Hampshire, Ann Hampshire, Mrs Su Lin (with daughter), Mrs Margaret Wolpe.

Many years later, Susan Hampshire was to write in her autobiography: 'My mother's decision not to send me to school in the ordinary way was, quite literally, my salvation'.

The Hampshire School soon became one which was approved of and admired by many people, willing and eager to entrust their children to its care. It has been said that the School had an air of magic, but perhaps it is more realistic to state that it possessed a charm and an intellectual vibrancy that was brought to it by those who taught there. There was constant artistic and intellectual stimulation and the quality of life (in and outside the classes) helped Miss Jane and Miss Ann, Miss Freda, Miss Shirley and others to enrich the lives of the pupils.

One of those pupils, Susan Stranks, remembers those days with affection and gratitude. She came from an artistic background – her father, Alan, was the creator of the very popular radio series 'P.C. 49' – and her parents were both understanding and supportive. For Susan, the School was 'a slightly fantasy world. We walked through Harrods to get to school, and we designed our own uniform and boaters. The School was in a church hall, and this made it like a village school in the middle of London.'

Susan remembers June Hampshire as a 'remarkable woman – perceptive, canny, wise and practical to a degree. I always thought there must be
something of the gypsy in her, for she was so knowing.' She recalls that 'it
was not a stage school in the usual sense. Our training helped us to understand that one could work through pain and discomfort when needed. We
received lots of real encouragement, and we learned tolerance and cour-
tesy. We were taught respect for everyone, including ourselves, and we also
learned that we must never be too frightened nor too proud even to do
the most menial tasks.'

In this child-centred society, the young pupils came to believe that
they could achieve whatever they wanted to achieve. June Hampshire
provided opportunity for all of her pupils. As
Susan Stranks says: 'If she felt we should
dance at the Royal Albert Hall, then she
would see to it that we *did* dance at the
Royal Albert Hall!'

The Royal Albert Hall was but one of
the places at which groups from The
Hampshire School appeared in those earlier
days. Concerts and shows abounded. On 25
July 1953, there was a *Coronation Matinée*
given by pupils at the Fortune Theatre,
Drury Lane. Susan Stranks delivered the
opening charity appeal and then played
Portia, with Carole Dowell as Nerissa and
Patricia Beckwith as a serving-maid in a
scene from *The Merchant of Venice*. Anthony
Dowell danced a tap solo, but he was not the
only child in the concert to become a ballet
star. Maina Gielgud, who was a courtier in

the playlet 'Blackbird Pie' in which Anthony played the King, was dancing with the Ballet du Marquis de Cuevas only nine years later. She then
spent periods with the London Festival Ballet and The Royal Ballet
before, in 1983, being appointed as Artistic Director of the Australian
National Ballet.

'Pas de deux' at the
Adelphi Theatre, 1955
– Jane Beyfus and
Anthony Dowell.

During the summer of 1954, June Hampshire took a group of senior pupils to the USA to dance and demonstrate at the American Dance Congress. The group included Ann Hampshire, Susan Hampshire, Patricia Beckwith, Gylda Bunday, Carole Dowell and Gail Horsfall. Carole Dowell followed a career in dancing before marrying and settling in California. Her younger brother, Anthony, was a remarkably gifted dancer, and June insisted that he attended an audition to qualify for the Royal Ballet School when he was eleven years of age. June was delighted when he was accepted. He became one of England's greatest classical ballet dancers. He is now Director of The Royal Ballet. In 1995 he was knighted for his services to dance.

Susan Stranks' love of the arts took her to St Martin's College and to The Royal Academy of Dramatic Art. She became the presenter of the children's television series 'Magpie' for many years. She now writes programmes for radio. She married the noted writer, musicologist and broadcaster Robin Ray. Her affection for the School has not lessened with the years – 'such a happy place,' she says, 'devoted to developing the positive'.

Outward bound for the USA in 1954. Outside the Hall – Gail Horsfall and Patricia Beckwith (back row), Gylda Bunday, Susan Hampshire and Carole Dowell (front row).

During the 1950s, June Hampshire also established ballroom–dancing classes during the Easter and Christmas holidays. For a decade, these were recognised and commented upon by such journals as *The Tatler*, *Illustrated London News* and *Harpers & Queen* as 'The Young People's Social Events of the Year'.

1954 and 1955 saw the school and dancing pupils combine again to stage *A Christmas Matinée* at the Adelphi Theatre in the Strand in aid of The Forces Help Society and Lord Roberts Workshops. Others to appear in that show were Miss Jane's daughter Eve Box–Grainger. Even Miss Jane's husband was recruited and he made an impressive Father Christmas!

At the Scala Theatre, Eve was joined by her brother Paul in another charity concert entitled *More Airs and Graces*. The opening scene was a lively and dashing czardas performed by Patricia Beckwith, Jane Beyfus, Gylda Bunday, Carole Dowell, Anna Goodman, Susan Hampshire, Sally Masser, Grace Ann Schweitzer and Susan Stranks.

Holiday ballroom–dancing classes and parties took place from 1953 to 1961 and were held variously at the Blue Pool (Dolphin Square), Crosby Hall (Chelsea) and the Anglo-Belgian Club (Belgrave Square). Pictured here in 1955 are (seated left to right) Cecil Orr, OBE, Jane Box-Grainger, Christopher Box-Grainger and Mrs Helen Beckwith, with Susan Hampshire and Sarah Searight (holding the cake).

RIGHT: New Airs and Graces at the Scala Theatre, London, 1955 – (left to right) Catherine Fuller, Paul Box-Grainger, Eve Box-Grainger, Nicola Fox-Linton, Nigel Turley, Babbie Shamsher, Catherine Lasselle.

RIGHT: New Airs and Graces at the Scala Theatre, London, 1955 – (left to right) Catherine Fuller, Paul Box-Grainger, Eve Box-Grainger, Nicola Fox-Linton, Nigel Turley, Babbie Shamsher, Catherine Lasselle.

BELOW: *New Airs and Graces*, Scala Theatre – Paul and Eve Box-Grainger.

All of these many and varied concerts and recitals throughout London and Surrey helped to raise much-needed monies for charities such as The Red Cross, Invalid Children's Aid Association, Women's Voluntary Services, and Save The Children Fund. They also provided valuable experience for some who were to find careers in the arts. Young people stood upon the stages of public theatres for the first time, and learned a great deal about deportment and presentation. Among others who benefited from their experience were Lavinia Bertram, Brian Carroll, Anita Finch, Alison Frazer, Susie Fletcher (stage name – Susannah York), Gillian McIver, Nicola Novello-Hunt, Susan Porrett and Elwyn Stock. Some years on, during the reign of Miss Jane, more pupils came to prominence in the theatre – Timothy Douglas, Belinda Hawke (now Belinda Lang), Juliet Hetreed, Fuschia Peters, Tahnee and Damon Welch, Charles Simpson, Linnet Taylor, Anoushka Menzies, Josephine and Monika Russell – while Olinda Fehr became a well-known author and columnist, and Natasha Mayersberg is making a name for herself in film production.

Inevitably, the years had begun to take their toll of June Hampshire. She had, almost single-handed, brought up four children and worked with unrelenting vigour for more than 32 years. She announced in November 1960 that she wished to retire and that she was going to close The Hampshire School. This announcement produced very different reactions from the family who were, in the main, pursuing personal goals: Susan had embarked on a glittering career in the theatre, films and television; John was engaged in a business career in Spain and Austria; while Ann and Jane reacted to their mother's announcement in contrasting ways. Ann had recently married David Sharp, and the likely closure of the School came almost as a relief – enabling her to enjoy a new life and to concentrate on raising a family.

Jane, however, saw her mother's decision as a catastrophe, and a complete waste of more than 30 years of dedicated hard work. She refused to allow the School to die. Her belief in the School, its aims, principles and special atmosphere, had persuaded her to abandon a promising stage career and return to teaching. Her own three children had received their early education at the School – leading to Eve winning an open scholarship to S. Michael's, Petworth; Paul's easy acceptance by Durston House prior to attending Tonbridge School; and Jill winning an exhibition to St Felix, Southwold. Her husband, Christopher, a multi-talented man with much business experience and energy, not only was supportive but shared her enthusiasm for the School.

Jane was adamant that the School should survive and, as from January 1961, an arrangement was reached whereby June would relinquish the post of Principal and financial management of the School. She would continue to teach within, and outside, the School for as long as possible – and she would act as Honorary Principal, so that her great experience would not be lost. Jane would become the new Principal, with sole responsibility for all educational and financial management. Meanwhile, Ann had refused the post of joint Head offered by her mother, in order to devote herself to her family without the burden of school duties and responsibilities.

This arrangement was reached amicably, since no problems arose within the family as to any division of property or capital and assets. Indeed, The Hampshire School was almost totally lacking in material assets.

Certainly, it was a popular decision with parents, pupils and staff when it was announced that Miss Jane was to become the new Principal – although there was sadness that the legendary June Hampshire would no longer have direct contact with many of them. All were pleased that The Hampshire School would continue as before. Not only would it continue but, as we shall see, it would grow and flourish.

The second phase of its history was at an end – a third, exciting period of development was to begin.

Mena El Din, aged 7.
('The Toy Shop', a ballet choreographed by June Hampshire, featured in many school concerts over the years.)

Miss Jane

In her capacity as Principal and Headmistress, 'Miss Jane' brought to the School a renewed vigour and confidence, allied to a realistic sense of business. Responsibility had long been part of her life and she was (and is still) blessed with great energy and a decisive mind combined with an air of quiet and controlled authority. In her autobiography, Susan Hampshire gave a perceptive appraisal of her sister:

Portrait by David Kemp, ARA.
Eve Box-Grainger, at 11 years of age, wins the first academic scholarship from the School to St Michael's School at Petworth, in 1964. Eve is pictured here (on the right) with her mother, sister Jill and brother Paul.

'Jane, the eldest, was an amazingly positive and patient sister – with the plaited auburn-gold hair of a girl in a medieval painting. It appeared to me at that time Jane found it impossible to fail an exam, impossible not to win first prize or be anywhere but top of her class. Without fuss or sentiment, she put herself in charge of the Hampshire offsprings and led us boldly.'

In similar manner, Jane put herself in charge of The Hampshire School and led it boldly. Her mother's retirement was to last barely five years – after much suffering, she died in March 1967 mourned by all with whom she had come in contact. There were generous tributes to her in *The Times* and *The Dance Journal*. It was tragic that she did not live to witness the great oak that her eldest daughter reared from the powerful acorn she had planted.

Despite the excellent reputation of the School, Jane did not inherit the easiest of tasks. When she took over management of the School in 1961, the number of pupils on roll undergoing full-time education was 41, with seven other pupils receiving dancing training only. Many of these 48 children had been granted 'special status', which meant that they received some concessions regarding fees. There was little or no equipment, and no premises with security of tenure. Furthermore, there was no profitability. No income was being generated that could be ploughed back into the School to help modernisation of its facilities. Miss Jane tells of the problems that faced her:

'Many people not connected directly with the School asked me why I had ever embarked upon such a demanding and arduous task. I had many reasons for doing so; not the least being my objection to seeing so many years of hard work wasted. I had a deep concern for the children still in classes in the Hall, and for the parents who had entrusted those children to our care. There was, too, a matter of family pride plus a strong belief that the School was (and is) an asset to Knightsbridge and the surrounding area. But the most important reason of all was that I felt that there was something magical about our little school. Even when the School was in its infancy, I was touched by that

The School went through a period of deep mourning on the death of Mrs June Hampshire in March 1967. This obituary was printed in *The Dance Journal,* and a tribute appeared in *The Times.*

IMPERIAL SOCIETY OF TEACHERS OF DANCING
DANCE JOURNAL", Spring 1967

Mrs. June Hampshire

of Carlisle Place, S.W.1. on 20th March following a severe illness.

Mrs. Hampshire was born in London on 20th August, 1902, the youngest of six children, and the only daughter, of a solicitor.

Although she trained with Euphan MacLaren and loved dancing, her family were very much against dancing as a career—considering it " not a profession for ladies "! She possessed an ideal figure for a ballerina, but family opposition prevented her from commencing the necessary training at a sufficient early date. Nevertheless, she appeared in a number of musicals, plays, and other productions in London—and also danced with the Opera Ballet at Covent Garden. She left the theatre in May 1925 to marry G. K. Hampshire, a rising young research chemist.

In 1928, June Hampshire started teaching dancing in Surrey, where she lived. She studied ballroom dancing with Alex Moore and became a Fellow of the Ballroom Branch. Later on, she became a member of the Cecchetti Branch and of the R.A.D. She opened her own studio in Basil Street, Knightsbridge in 1932 under the name of The Jane Ann School of Dancing. She received much help from Anton Dolin, who taught in the studio. During the war she was assisted regularly by Vera Volkova. In the latter part of the war Mrs. Hampshire joined the W.A.A.F. and served at a fighter aerodrome in Scotland.

In 1945, she realised a long-standing ambition and founded The Hampshire School—a school which provided a full academic education integrated with all forms of dancing. The school flourished and is now extremely well known—Susannah York, Anthony Dowell, Susan Stranks, and Alison Frazer being but a few of her pupils. She continued to expand her interests in dancing, and became a Member of both the National and Scottish Country Dance Branches.

In 1961, she relinquished direct administrative control of the school in order to devote more time to her first love—teaching and dancing. Many hundreds of young people attended her ballroom classes and formal dances, and she was noted for the hard work and help she gave to childrens' charities.

In 1964, very shortly after his retirement as a Director of Imperial Chemical Industries Ltd., her husband died. She continued to teach in London and Folkestone until January 1966, when she was forced to enter hospital and undergo a severe operation. She appeared to make a good recovery but, in September of last year, suffered a relapse and grew steadily weaker. With typical courage and charm, she fought her illness to the very end—but eventually passed peacefully away.

June Hampshire is survived by a son, three daughters, and seven grandchildren. Her eldest daughter (Mrs. Jane Box-Granger) has been Head of the School since 1961—and her youngest daughter is the well known stage and film actress, Susan Hampshire. A sweet and genuine person, Mrs. Hampshire will be remembered with great affection by her many friends both within and outside the Society.

"magic" – a very special quality arising initially from my mother's unique personality, and something so hard to define as the School grew and grew. That magical feeling had persuaded me to give up a career in the theatre to resume teaching – a decision I never regretted – and I know that the same "magic" has more or less touched every one of our pupils through the years. As one listens to people recounting stories of their schooldays, one realises that many have not been so fortunate in his or her education.'

While jealously guarding the distinctive atmosphere of the School, Jane was faced with the problems of improving the premises and the basic need to introduce new and modern subjects – widening the opportunities offered to pupils.

Lucinda Chambers, now fashion editor of *Vogue*, was one of the pupils at the School during this transitional period. She recalls: 'I think that I was sent to the School because my brother was a good dancer, and I followed in his wake. I remember that each class was sat round its own table. I was kept down for a time because I talked too much and because my friend, Amynta Cardwell, was always singing opera! The School was so relaxed and so wonderfully happy.'

Lucinda found her own freedom of expression at the School, and through studying later at Hornsey Art College, but she does remember one sad time at school. She writes:

'My brother had a friend, Johnny Deakin, who died tragically of cancer at the age of nine. My parents asked if they could give a cup in his memory and Miss Jane agreed; deciding that the cup should be given each year for "effort and progress". It was won first by Timmy Loder, a little boy who was autistic, and his parents were so thrilled. They thought that it was the very best thing that had ever happened to Timmy.'

The happy atmosphere and vigorous work ethic of the School were maintained, but Miss Jane had other problems to consider:

Members of the Upper School staff in 1975 – Mrs D. Boulton, Mrs Judith Wood, Miss Barbara, Miss Louisa, Miss Sheila, Miss Fawzia, Miss Laura, Miss Wendy, Miss Christine, Miss Anne (Butterfield), Miss Jane, Lady Lisle, Miss Deirdre, Mrs G. Brampton.

'My mother's former staff – Miss Freda, Miss Shirley, Mrs Betty Peck and Gordon Taylor – remained in the School, but replacements for my mother and sister Ann had to be found. Lady Lisle was engaged to teach English, history, French and scripture – a most happy choice for she continued to teach in the School for more than 30 years. Miss Anne Butterfield, a highly experienced Montessori teacher, took over the Kindergarten children, teaching them to read, write and to master numbers – another very happy choice. All these teachers were much loved by the children, some staying at the School long after normal retirement age. I have to say that the sheer experience of teachers past retirement age can be invaluable to young teachers, as well as to the pupils.'

During this period of reorganisation and development, Miss Jane's husband, Christopher Box-Grainger, was a tower of strength in the manner in which he supported his wife in her efforts. Although he had the demands of his own highly successful career, he worked almost every

weekend on administrative matters as part-time bookkeeper, financial
adviser, bursar and secretary. He drew up the original prospectus which
set out very clearly the School's objectives and programmes. This successful publication is worthy of quotation today as an example of Miss Jane's
educational philosophy:

> 'The children learn to work and play without unnecessary rules or
> undue discipline. More than usual care is taken by the Principal and
> Staff to ensure that they learn to show thought and respect for others
> at all times. Emphasis is placed on the importance of poise and
> deportment, in order that pupils will be given confidence when even-
> tually becoming full members of society.
>
> Special care and attention is given to all pupils who find academic
> work difficult or who, for various reasons, have missed much basic
> instruction. Every help and encouragement is offered to such pupils
> to help them to make up for lost time, and thus regain confidence in
> a happy atmosphere.'

The former open-plan layout of St Saviour's Hall, once seen as something of a disadvantage, was now regarded as a distinct advantage – the
'new look' of open and integrated design which came to popularity in
the 1960s. The Hall was, of course, readily adaptable to this 'new look' in
education – it had always been present! – but new equipment and facilities had to be funded from the Box-Graingers' own resources. Over a
period of less than ten years, there were many improvements – new
cloakrooms and hand basins, the kitchen was refurbished, new lockers and
furniture were brought into use, electrical heating installed, telephones
connected, the Hall redecorated completely, while a new and comprehensive range of text and work books was introduced.

The demand for places grew and, within three years, the Hall
was accommodating over 80 pupils between the ages of three and 16
years. There was a long waiting-list of those wishing to attend the School.
The intense activity of the average schoolday had to be seen to be
believed.

The pupils would assemble for a hymn, the Lord's Prayer and a few words from Miss Jane. This assembly would be followed by exercises to music. The tables were then set up, books were taken from lockers and the classes would sit at some six or seven long tables for lessons to begin at 9.30 a.m. At 11.00 a.m., there would be a break for a quarter of an hour when the children played in the central area of the Hall. There were further lessons until 12.30 p.m., when the small children left for their homes.

The tables were cleared of books and covered with cloths, to allow the remaining pupils to eat lunch in their normal form places. After lunch, the middle and senior groups were led in 'crocodiles' to Hyde Park for rounders, or to a local swimming pool, or to gather for attending dancing and handicraft classes. There were activities of every kind, much cheerful bustle and laughter, with the careful organisation required – all supervised by members of the staff at all times.

Exciting as open-plan teaching was, it raised certain problems, as Miss Jane remembers:

'As the ages of the children ranged from three to 16 years, there were difficulties regarding noise and in syllabus planning – not to mention the construction of timetables! This was achieved by fine teamwork from the staff, absolutely essential at any time but more so when operating in an open-plan situation. Although we had always operated the method, the numbers now attending demanded timetabling of almost military precision. But the benefits to the children in a well-operated open-plan environment are many. The needs of each individual child can be seen quickly and be fulfilled much more easily than in a conventional classroom structure. The children enjoyed a family atmosphere – big children mixing, talking, playing and working happily alongside the very young children. Tolerance, kindness and discipline from each pupil was essential and these values were absorbed daily and by habit.'

During this period, the academic achievements of the School gave ample testimony to the success of the system and the fine teamwork of the staff. Between 1961 and 1969 scholarships were gained to the City of

Skiing at Alpbach, Austria, in 1965. The party includes Miranda Banks, Eve Box-Grainger, Jill Box-Grainger, Paul Box-Grainger, Charlotte Du Cann, Martin Grogan, Katherine Henry, Christina Loder, Timothy Loder, Mrs Inge Loder, Christine Montanari, Ivan Montanari, Stephanie Morgan, Nicola Novello-Hunt, Deborah Tapley, Penelope Thomson, Alexander Wax, Mrs Thelma Wax.

London School for Girls, S. Michael's School at Petworth and St Felix School at Southwold. Almost 100% success was recorded for pupils sitting the Common Entrance and Eleven-Plus examinations during the period.

In themselves, these successes created further problems in that the demand for places grew enormously, and the waiting-list became longer and longer. The need for much larger premises was obvious, and Miss Jane decided that she must take action to make it possible to accommodate more pupils. She set up a Building Committee to meet once a month during 1966.

This committee was chaired by Anthony Ashton, then financial director of Esso Petroleum, and included some notable people – General Ian Graeme, David Donaldson, Richard Du Cann, Mrs Dorothy Henry, the Hon. Christopher Loder (now Lord Wakehurst), Arthur Rodwell (the family accountant) and Jane herself. With the exception of Arthur Rodwell, all members of the committee were parents of current or former pupils of the School. Most of them also had personal connections with the Hampshire family.

Miss Jane hunted for a building in the Knightsbridge area and found No. 63 Ennismore Gardens – a late 19th-century five-storey house facing north over Princes Gardens to Hyde Park – and set in a safe cul-de-sac eminently suitable for the setting down and collection of schoolchildren. The committee was asked to consider acquisition of the building, which was up for sale. It was then known as Cowie House, owned by a Mrs Candler, who had already been granted planning permission by Westminster City Council to run a small nursery school, while she and her family lived in the upper part of the house. The house was on offer at £46,000 freehold.

After much deliberation, the committee decided that the income and accounts of the School at the time could not meet and sustain a freehold purchase of about £46,000 – plus the costs for conversion and modernisation. Miss Jane was devastated. She says:

'I could not believe that friends could be so short-sighted as to turn down the freehold purchase of a house already used as a school, and situated in one of the smartest areas of London. As a freehold price, £46,000 seemed almost ridiculously cheap for, even in 1966, it was safe to assume that the building would increase in value quite rapidly. The house was not perfect, but it provided a thousand times better facilities and potential than St Saviour's Hall – crammed as it was with more than eighty pupils. We estimated that the necessary modernisation could bring the cost up to between £68,000 and £70,000, but even then, I felt the acquisition would be a bargain. I was bitterly disappointed.'

It has never been a characteristic of the Hampshire family to accept defeat. However, two years later, in 1968, Mrs Candler wrote to Miss Jane offering her the building at the lower price of £45,000 and she decided to adopt different tactics. She and her husband hurriedly called a meeting with their new accountant, Alan Fabes, introduced by Sir Charles Russell, to plan as to how the building could be purchased without further discussion with the committee.

Alan Fabes proposed that The Hampshire School should be turned into a private limited company, and that Miss Jane personally should purchase the building. The School would then rent the building from Miss Jane under a ten-year contract. Alan Fabes, Sir Charles Russell and Leonard Biggs (the family insurance broker) then put the scheme into operation and contracts were exchanged in December 1968 at the lower price of £43,500. Miss Jane's dream of a new and larger Hampshire School was close to realisation.

The School would always be protected by its new limited company status, but this brave and innovative business plan was not without its humorous side. It was discovered that the new School company could not be registered as The Hampshire School Limited, for a driving school in the county of Hampshire had already claimed that title. So, after much research, the company was registered in 1969 as Hampshire Tutorials Limited – with Miss Jane appointed chairman and managing director and Christopher Box-Grainger as company secretary and director. Later on, the children of the Box-Graingers (Eve, Paul and Jill) were to join the Board with Arthur Rodwell.

The building had been secured and parents informed, but gigantic problems remained. There were just over three weeks before the start of the January 1970 term, and there was a huge amount of reconstruction work to be done. Miraculously, quite a lot of it was completed by architect John Gray, the City of Westminster surveyor and teams of builders who worked very long hours in the short time available. Their tasks included the construction of a new internal staircase to comply with fire regulations, new assembly and dining halls, kitchen, removal of all internal walls on four floors to provide large classrooms, new lavatories and wash-basins, cloakrooms, a staff room and two offices, rewiring and replumbing and painting throughout. Then came the installation of new ancillary services such as fire detection equipment and alarms, telephone system, clock and class signal system, new floor coverings and furnishings, and many other details.

To complete all of this work in just over three weeks proved to be an impossibility, but much of it was finished. The basement was not ready, and the new external fire escape to connect the first and fourth floors could not be engineered until the end of the Easter holiday.

However, all this work did not prevent the Common Entrance examinations taking place in March 1970 – places being won by Miranda Banks to Downe House, Sabeeha Noorani to the City of London School for Girls, Nicola Steel to the Francis Holland School, Nicolas Humphris and Alexander Ward-Jackson to Westminster Under School. All normal school activities continued successfully, although there were some unforseen interruptions and anxieties. On three occasions, the basement was flooded; this was discovered finally to have been caused by pigeons' nests in the roof area! Miss Jane wrote: 'One has almost forgotten that the external fire escape had to be carried through the building, girder by girder, and during its erection we were forbidden to look out through the rear windows in case the glare from the welders' blow-torches affected our eyes!' By December 1970, the new school building was operating smoothly but nothing of the old sense of 'magic' had been lost in the new and larger surroundings, and all of the former principles had been retained.

That these principles and the distinct character of the School survived, in an educational climate becoming increasingly pressurised and

Upper School staff in 1974 – Mrs Judith Wood, Miss Barbara, Miss Laura, Miss Dierdre, Miss Fawzia, Mrs D. Boulton, Miss Christine, Miss Winnie, Miss Anne (Butterfield), Miss Jane, Lady Lisle, Miss Alice, Miss Wendy.

Candidates for the Common Entrance examination from the Upper School in 1981 (with Lady Lisle, seated centre) – (back row) Tara Capon, Zainab Al Atia, Ana Maria Wormald and Yasmin Mahzari, (front row) Anna Bevan, Emma Gold, Sherine Shaker and Fleur Montanaro.

demanding, is a testimony to the quality and integrity of Miss Jane and her staff. The Box-Graingers themselves were well aware of the educational pressures faced by parents and their children. Their own three children had passed through their public schools and were applying for university places. They were conscious of the fears of many parents: the fear that their children were engaged in a perpetual race. However happy and settled a child is at preparatory school, not all can cope with the current fierce and relentless competition beyond that stage.

With 130 pupils now in attendance, The Hampshire School faced this situation with typical courage. Miss Jane was determined that neither competition nor pressure should dilute the School's principles and ethos:

'It is not easy to maintain the "magic" when one realises that the curriculum of a preparatory school is confined by the syllabus of Common Entrance and Eleven-Plus examinations – examinations through which the major proportion of candidates must pass to move on to senior schools. Failure of a child to pass Common Entrance generates fear in the minds of most parents — a fear exacerbated by the Heads of many senior schools whose lists are allegedly always over-flowing and who state that it would be difficult for any child to enter their schools without a good Common Entrance pass. This fear, fuelled by some Heads of senior schools and the gossip among some parents and friends, has prevented a number of preparatory schools from expanding their curricula sufficiently into creative and artistic activities — so essential to the production of a well-educated, fully rounded and informed human being.'

However, due to the high costs of fitting out and equipping 63 Ennismore Gardens, as well as the considerable personal investment involved, the School suffered a cash-flow crisis. Miss Jane writes:

'I was uncertain as to how to deal with this problem and we consulted an old family friend well versed in church property and administrative matters, the Reverend Patrick Hewat, who had christened my three children. I shall never cease to be grateful for his practical advice and assistance, and he then gave his time for the next two years by acting as the School's bursar. He figures very high indeed in the list of friends of the School.'

None of the building works and temporary financial problems affect-ed the continuing academic success. In addition, the programme of arts subjects and sport thrived — dance, drama, music, art and handicrafts were as firmly placed within the timetable as always. After the move of the Upper School to Ennismore Gardens in 1970, the very first issue of the School magazine records that 50 pupils were successful in the Cecchetti ballet examinations; 26 pupils were awarded medals for Scottish country dancing with 42 younger pupils receiving test certificates; 15 pupils gained 27 medals for skiing during the visit to Austria; and the junior and senior cups for swimming were won by Sheran Thomas and Deborah Tapley respectively in the School's first swimming gala. Miss Jane writes: 'These activities are very important in the development of courage, character and confidence – especially if care is taken to ensure a reasonably high rate of success, without reduction of standards.'

The academic year ended with the concert and prizegiving at the Dorchester Hotel in Park Lane. In the School magazine, Charlotte Lyon of the Remove form writes:

'It was a beautiful day and the sun was hot. Everybody was very excited and charged into the changing rooms. The Dorchester rang with excitement and everybody jumped about, then began to get dressed into their costumes. Miss Jane came in and told us to be quiet and hurry up. We were ready quite soon and lined up for the opening procession. As we came out and into the Ballroom, we all began to be frightened and I noticed some people went bright red! After that was over, the rest of the concert went very quickly and well. Some people went wrong in places but I think that went unnoticed. "Alice in Wonderland" was great fun and went very well. When the concert was over, the parents and children all had tea, juice and jelly to eat. After that and the prizes, all the parents went to have sherry and their daughters and sons joined them. We said goodbye to each other and to the teachers, happy that it was all over and nothing more to worry about!'

The involvement of parents is a very important part of any school's existence. The new building allowed the introduction of the first of many evening receptions for parents, when they could speak with the staff about their children and meet other parents. A pupil's progress could be discussed in confidence, questions regarding the basic curriculum and activities answered and, if any, problems solved. The parents of pupils at The Hampshire School were helpful in supporting the School in many ways. In an attempt to raise money for the building fund, some of them gave permission for their daughters to appear in the film *Isadora*, which starred Vanessa Redgrave and was directed by Karel Reisz. Lucinda Chambers was cast as Deirdre, the daughter of Isadora Duncan and Gordon Craig. The film was a huge success, and it was shot in several locations – including the Rothschild mansion of Waddesdon Manor and South Lodge, Knightsbridge.

The School magazine also records much help from parents. Derith Mullins (age 11) writes: 'During the Spring Term, the former staff room was full of workmen, tools and odd pieces of wood. Now that room is a laboratory with a sink, blackboard, charts and shelves. Round two sides of the room are built-in cabinets with cupboards and drawers full of test tubes, and other scientific instruments. We like working in the lab, and the staff are happy with their new

room, new armchairs and carpet.' Nearly £500 was raised by the parents at a bazaar to help fund the new science laboratory. Nicola Weir (age 10) writes: 'We had money very kindly given to the School by Mrs I. T. Logie,

ABOVE: Vanessa Redgrave with (from left to right) Ruth Du Cann, Lucinda Chambers and Tracy Maconochie, just a few of the pupils who appeared with her in the major film production of *Isadora*. Lucinda Chambers, now fashion editor of *Vogue*, was cast as Deirdre, Isadora Duncan's child by Gordon Craig.

LEFT: The filming of *Isadora* in the grounds of Waddesdon Manor. Vanessa Redgrave with pupils of the School, including Felice de Smet, Charlotte Du Cann, Angela Duvollet-Lynch, Tracy Maconochie.

Pupils at work in the library in 1983, including Roula Abusamra, Olivia Campbell, Adriana Cassandro, Rowan Douglas, Charlotte Fooks, Bahar Ghaffari, Caroline Marris, Iona McCorquodale, Fiona McOran Campbell, Isabel Olive, Stasha Palos, Catherine Peppiatt, Fuschia Peters, Jeannette Platou, Josephine Russell, Shahpari Shahandeh, Nicola West, Jessica Wilson.

Mrs. J. Gore, Mr and Mrs Gwilliam, Mr and Mrs Hunter, the Kobe Bank, Mrs T. Porterfield and Mrs C. Speed to buy books for our Library. This helped us buy more than a hundred and seventy new books – big ones, small ones, fat ones, thin ones all about history, science and all kinds of things, including a number of fiction books. We have a real system now, with cards and a date stamp to go with it.' The support and kindness of parents took many forms. For example, Mr Josef Shaftel arranged for Form IVB to visit the film set of *Alice's Adventures in Wonderland* at Shepperton Studios. Iselin Remoy (age 10) writes: 'A coach came to pick us up from School and when we arrived at Shepperton, a lady showed us around. We saw the White Rabbit's house and the Pool of Tears; the scenery was beautiful and very well made. We had our photo taken with Fiona Fullerton (Alice) and Michael Crawford (the White Rabbit) under the big mushroom where the Caterpillar sits. We had a lovely day and got back to the School around 3.30 p.m. I think it was very kind of Mr Shaftel to invite us to Shepperton Studios.' The generosity of another parent, Frederick Brogger (father of Christine and Karen), provided another cinematic occasion – all of the four top forms being taken to the Odeon Theatre, Leicester Square, to see his production of *Kidnapped*. Patsy Rubin reports in the magazine: 'It was a super film, with lots of blood-thirsty battles. The Scottish scenery was beautiful and the music was lovely, but sad!'

The regular support and encouragement of the parents was deeply appreciated by Miss Jane. She says: 'We cannot leave out Mrs Sheila Tapley, mother of Deborah, whose assistance in the move from St Saviour's Hall to Ennismore Gardens was really invaluable. She then volunteered to work in the School as its secretary, and did so for a number of years – when her tact, loyalty and skill in dealing with parents were a tremendous asset.'

The popularity of the School with parents drawn from the world of films and television would have pleased June Hampshire. It was kind of Richard Goodwin, for example, father of Jason and Sabine, to arrange for the pupils to see the costumes and special screenings of his film *Tales of Beatrix Potter*. Ken Russell, father of Victoria, Michael Powell, father of Columba, and Raymond Harryhausen, father of Vanessa, and others also kindly contributed to the extraordinary cultural background of the School.

Stimulating and exciting as these special events were, there remained above all the simple enjoyment in the day-to-day routines of the School. Felicity Kirchner writes:

'On lovely sunny Tuesdays and Thursdays, Miss Jane lets us have picnic lunches in Hyde Park. Everybody looks forward to 12.40 p.m. when we put on our boaters and walk to the Park in pairs. When we get there, we pick up little bags of food and bottles of milk. We then sit in groups to eat lunch. We usually have an egg, a roll with ham, lettuce, tomato, crackers and an apple. When we have eaten this, we play on the grass before going back to school for lessons.'

A quarter of a century later, we can still taste the pleasure that all of these various excursions gave and the sense of 'belonging' and happiness that children had in being pupils of The Hampshire School. The School

Form IVA of the Upper School in 1971 – Miss Helen with Alexandra Blaker, Victoria Broackes, Christine Brogger, Charlotte Dudley-Smith, Ruth Du Cann, Christina Fransioli, Juliet Hetreed, Kath Hunter, Marina Logie, Bridget Penney, Pamela Pope, Susanna Remoy, Caroline Steel.

bubbled with life, and every year the magazine reported another innovation – the first BAGA gymnastic awards, the first music concert, the first performance of plays in French, the first string quintet (organised by Mrs Phibbs), the first art exhibition (brilliantly organised by Mrs Judith Wood), the first National Dancing displays, the first play and verse competition, formation of the First Brompton Pack of Brownies at the School, and much else besides.

Formation of the Brownie Pack was prompted by Miss Jane's long-standing interest in the Girl Guide movement. At her schools in Surrey and North Wales, she had been a keen Guide and Patrol Leader – and she was persuaded to become the Commissioner of the Kensington and Chelsea Division of the Girl Guides. With her many and various duties with the School and charity work, one wonders how she could find any time at all to undertake another quite onerous task – but, typically, she did so with much success for six years.

Not all of the innovations were an immediate success, when it came to netball and rounders with other schools and the staff. In 1972, Maclise Macomber wrote of the first interschool netball match: 'Falkner House challenged Forms IVA and Remove to a match. It was a disaster! We lost 3–13, but we thoroughly enjoyed it.' The following year, the pupils took on the staff at rounders and, as Alexandra Shaftel reported, the result followed the pattern set by the netball players against Falkner House: 'On 10th July, we played the staff at rounders. We fielded well but when it came to batting, the teachers caught us out. The staff won, but it was a very enjoyable match.'

The reputation of the School grew and grew, as did the profusion of external activities which undoubtedly helped to publicise The Hampshire School. The School was always in the news throughout the 1970s. Mrs Peter Rogers of the Women's Royal Voluntary Service (WRVS) chose a dozen pupils to model clothes that had been made from out-of-date garments and unwanted furnishings. The fashion show was a national event, and pictures of the girls appeared in many newspapers and magazines, including *The Daily Telegraph* and *Country Life*. Then the School was featured on BBC television in a series presented by Valerie Singleton, called 'Val Meets the VIPs'. In 1974, the VIP in question was Susan Hampshire – who was taken back to The Hampshire School, to be seen with pupils leaving the school bus, in the cloakrooms, playing recorders and taking part in a National Dancing class.

Would-be botanists caring for the patio garden, 1983 – Rowan Douglas, Claudine Moss, Catherine Peppiatt, Shahpari Shahandeh.

Parallel with this hive of activity, the physical development continued apace. A new central heating system was installed in St Saviour's Hall. Ennismore Gardens saw the building of a patio garden outside Miss Jane's office, while a new pottery kiln was fitted in the basement.

One wonders at the sheer energy of it all. On top of all the visits and excursions, concerts and host of other activities, the highest academic standards were being maintained. And even Falkner House was now being beaten at netball! There was a tremendous vitality driving through the place, and Mrs Dorothy Ind remembers how she came into contact with the School.

At the Arts Educational School at Tring, Dorothy Ind had been an outstanding teacher of dance to children who were to make their names in ballet and theatre, but she was now married with two young sons. Her husband is a doctor and one of his colleagues, Dr Newton, recommended The Hampshire School highly – his own children, Clare and James, being pupils at St Saviour's Hall. So Charles and Thomas Ind became pupils at the School.

Dorothy was immediately impressed by how well everything was done and she recalls:

'Miss Jane ran Scottish country dancing classes twice a week in the basement hall. It was taken very seriously, and we took exams and gave little concerts. I wasn't allowed to take the exams because I was a professional, but I took part in all the demonstrations with my partner, Mrs Jane Prior. I don't think that Miss Jane was altogether happy with the ballet examination results being achieved at the time. She was always determined that everyone should reach her or his full potential, and invited me out to lunch at the Hurlingham Club. It was a beautiful sunny day and we had a delightful lunch looking out over the gardens, croquet lawns and tennis courts of that renowned club. Then she drove me back to Chelsea and, on that journey, she invited me to come and teach ballet at her school. I said that I couldn't as I had two young children and that I had no intention of teaching again. She persisted, and asked me to set down my terms and conditions. When I didn't write, she phoned me and, when I finally sent a note, she accepted my terms without question.

That's how I came to teach ballet at The Hampshire School, and I've never regretted it. The children were very rewarding to teach – in fact, I would say that they were the best I ever had. Miss Jane resurrected my career, and I am now involved with 32 institutions including The Hampshire School.

Miss Jane had the capacity for making things happen. I remember that we were due to give a concert at St Columba's in Pont Street. We had the dress rehearsal in the morning to give the performance in the afternoon – the rehearsal was total chaos. I felt that the afternoon must turn into a disaster, and I didn't want my dancers to be part of it. The little ones were doing a French play, and didn't seem to have the slightest idea of what was going on – I was most embarrassed. But the performance in the afternoon was incredible. Miss Jane just took over. She led the little ones on to the stage and told them where to stand to deliver the play. She directed affairs in a masterly manner, and the concert was a roaring success.

It was a wonderful school to choose for dancing and drama, but it also built up the pupils in every respect. In the Kindergarten, the children sat at communal tables and my elder son learned to read quite fluently by the age of three. He was taught by Miss Anne Butterfield – a wonderful teacher.'

This is a commendation that Miss Jane herself echoes for, to her, the teaching of reading was of paramount importance. She had witnessed the pain that reading problems can cause at school, and beyond school. Miss Jane says:

'I was very concerned when I saw that my youngest sister, Susan, was having reading difficulties. I was a teacher of the older children in the School during Susan's formative years, and was in an admirable position to observe the problem arising and the likely solutions – another advantage of an open-plan school. So, when I became Principal of the School, I was insistent that all the children in my care would learn to read and write well and at the correct ages.

Depending on the ability of individual pupils, the normal age for mastering the skill of reading is between four and seven years. I am proud to say that, during my more than 25 years as Headmistress, we did not produce a single pupil who started to learn to read and write

Group I of the Lower School in 1974 – Miss Susan with Paige Baird, Benjamin Ball, Richard Binstock, Zoltan Bozoky, Lisa Branch, Sophie Burton, Jonathan Da Silva Clamp, Gabrielle Douthett, Lucy Earle, Annabel Garrow, Gabrielle Gourgey, Christopher Granier-Deferre, Charlotte Mallinson-Mathew, Conrad McDonnell, Lucy Morgan, Rana Nasir, Julie Parker, Asa Peronace, Roderic Puchner, Katie Sloan, Justine Suissa, James Tennant, Alice Todhunter, Louise Woodley.

in The Hampshire School who could be described as having lasting reading difficulties. I must emphasise that the early teaching of reading and writing is of the utmost importance, if a pupil is to avoid reading problems at a later stage. Here, it is appropriate that I pay a special word of thanks to Miss Anne Butterfield, a wonderful teacher, who helped the School to achieve this atypical result. I, and all of the pupils she taught, will always be grateful to her.

Strange though it may seem, the avoidance of reading problems begins with the teaching of handwriting. There are many different forms and styles of handwriting, but there is only one way to avoid pupils suffering from confusion. Each school *must* have a handwriting policy. If, for example, one looks at the lower case letter "t", one realises that there are at least six or seven styles of writing the letter. It is easy for an adult to recognise all the variations of "t", but a small child can find it very confusing. Therefore, it is essential that there is a co-ordinated programme of handwriting for *all* teachers. This means that there must be meetings to clarify that all members of staff are employing the letter formation chosen by the school. Having agreed a style of handwriting, it is now time to make sure that children form letters correctly. This can be a slow and rather laborious process for teachers but, for the children, it is the correct way of avoiding reading difficulties at a later stage.

Group II of the Lower School in 1975 – Miss Anthea with Richard Binstock, Sophie Brennan, Jake Deadman, Lucy Earle, Annabel Garrow, Christopher Granier-Deferre, Lawrence James, Rana Nasir, Keith Wilson.

It is preferable to begin with lower-case letters, naming them phonically, and then to introduce capital letters fairly quickly – using personal and adult names. It is necessary to introduce the capitals so that a child can write his or her own name correctly. Each separate letter must be demonstrated, showing pupils the starting point and how to complete the letter, starting at the top and continuing to finish the body of the letter, before adding horizontal strokes or dots. It is imperative that every letter is taught, guided and watched – so that no letter is reversed or begins in the wrong place. Pupils should be trained to read "flash cards" correctly *before* reading from books is introduced. We did not allow words and sentences to be copied without the strict monitoring of the formation of letters. Many reading difficulties can be put down to unsupervised copying at early stages.'

Miss Jane was ever methodical and determined in her approach, and her decisions were reached after much thought, observation and considerable research. Then the application was positive and disciplined.

The School at work in 1983 – Form I including Alexandra Zaphiriou, Jamie Grant Peterkin, Andrea Kleanthous, Kinda Kayyali, Michael Wild, Renée Searle and Arminé Guzelian, with Miss Elaine.

'English is a complicated language to read. One cannot read it phonetically and some words can only be read by recognition: i.e., the "look and say" method. The reading scheme chosen should be graded and, initially, have a limited vocabulary. It should include phonetically sounded words, with "look and say" words and flash cards with plenty of interesting repetition. The scheme should also contain a number of parallel readers for each stage which use the same vocabularies as the main reader. Repetition is extremely valuable in acquiring fluency. A disposable workbook on the reading scheme, in which to answer simple questions, makes for easier progress.

The teacher's rôle is very important. It must be one of continual encouragement and patience, regardless as to whether pupils are advancing quickly or slowly. A daily routine of "hearing" every pupil must be practised if maximum progress is to be attained. This practice requires some organisation and ingenuity by the teacher, especially when dealing with larger classes. Some children are naturally competitive, so a teacher needs to be fair and wise in the use of praise if confidence and industry are to be developed. It is essential that the teacher's attitude does not dampen the enthusiasm of the quickest and brightest while, at the same time, not demotivating the slower readers. This is not an easy task for any teacher.

I have a very real concern at the moment – that is, the use of the word "dyslexic", which one hears and reads everywhere these days. It has become the popular educational "buzz word", and I cannot but wonder if all of the children deemed to be dyslexic today are really suffering from "word blindness". I believe that labelling of young children in this fashion is counter-productive in many ways – leading to loss of self-confidence and happiness, particularly when the label suggests that they are inferior to their peers. To be considered as dyslexic hints (or is assumed by some) that a child is handicapped and, therefore, a kind of second-class person. This must be wrong. Before attaching this label to a pupil, has there been enough thorough examination of other possible reasons why the learning of reading, spelling and writing is blocked?

Wide experience of teaching young children prompts me to pose questions which many tend to avoid. For instance – are the reading schemes designed with sufficient care to overcome failing by pupils? Can we be sure that teachers are receiving sound training in the skills of instruction in the basics of reading? Is there any study regarding the current break-up of families or any such domestic problems which can seriously affect progress in reading? Do teachers today help parents to understand the best way to help their children in learning to read? Even more important in some cases, do teachers generate trust in parents by consistently good performance in this vital area?

We avoided reading problems at The Hampshire School by keeping to a strict system of careful teaching and monitoring of letter formation for beginners, and using phonetics and "look and say" methods for reading and writing. We had a definitive school reading and handwriting policy, which was checked at staff meetings every term. We used a good and proven reading scheme, with graded and parallel reading books and associated workbooks. We relied upon a patient and encouraging teaching staff, who heard young pupils read daily in a calm and unpressurised way. In order to discover any weaknesses unnoticed previously, there was additional monitoring of junior pupils by the Principal or Deputy Head – so as to apply suitable remedies as soon as possible. We also insisted that children learn to read at school and only when they could read confidently, were they allowed to take their reading books home.

This rigid adherence to a firm foundation in learning has been the great strength of the School – a foundation on which the later success of very many former pupils has been based. Perhaps all of this will be regarded as old-fashioned and redolent of earlier times – but it used to work very well and I can see no reason why the care I have referred to cannot work just as well in the 1990s.'

None of this, of course, can be achieved in full without the co-operation of parents – and, in 1976, the Parents' Association was formed. Organising coffee mornings and other functions, the committee introduced the parents of new pupils to each other and to the

Miss Doreen teaching Maths in 1983 to Form IIIB, including Natalie Alwan, Clarissa Box, Francesca Ingram, Tanya Kalla, Leila Lak, Guadalupe Latapi, Jessica Laurence, Philippa Milton, Amanda Neerman, Lisa Papadopoulous, Daniella Parrino, Merhnaz Sadati, Ashleigh Seagar, Alexandra Zaphiriou.

working patterns of the School, as well as arranging sales and purchase of second-hand uniform and leisure clothing. The Association was chaired for eighteen years by Frances Aitken with much success.

The School was approaching a period of celebration. The Queen's Silver Jubilee was welcomed in splendid style. An engraved pottery mug was given to all staff and pupils to commemorate the occasion, and a Jubilee collage was designed by Mrs Judith Wood, the art mistress. It was sewn by pupils, staff and some parents, and it hangs in the entrance hall of Ennismore Gardens to this day. Lessons in history and art were centred on the Queen's reign and on her ancestors. There were group visits to the Royal Academy, the National Gallery, the Tower of London, the Royal Hospital at

Celebration of Her Majesty The Queen's Silver Jubilee held in 1977. Parents and pupils throng the School's open day exhibition.

Chelsea, Kensington Palace, Buckingham Palace Mews, the Natural History and Science Museums – even the London Dungeon! There was a cruise along the Thames and a visit to the Victoria and Albert Museum to see the Royal Jubilee Cake and other delicacies made for the Jubilee celebrations. All of this was in preparation for the School's own contributions to the great day – which took the form of an open day exhibition attended by hundreds of parents, the Deputy Mayor of Kensington and Chelsea and the headmistresses of many other London schools. The exhibition was a tremendous success – the theme of the show being Her Majesty's Silver

Jubilee in the shapes of artwork, handicrafts, sewing, original poems, collections of newspaper and magazine cuttings, and a display of 'project' files. Prizes and special commendations were won by Anna Bevan, Eugenie Brown, Natacha du Pont de Bie, Louisa Greatrex, Philippa James, Samantha Keil, Victoria Knight, Michael Mackay-Lewis, Sophie McDonald Woods, Rebecca Mitchell, Emily Pinckney, Lisa Pinto, Angela Reissmann, Sandra Rosignoli, Rebecca Sparks, Samantha Suissa and Belinda Tee. The Jubilee festival included sport – at netball, the School succeeded in beating Falkner House and Queen's Gate School, while beating the 'Old Girls' at rounders as well! In addition, there was a sponsored walk around the Serpentine in Hyde Park to raise funds for the Prince Charles Jubilee Fund for Youth – one circuit being approximately 2½ miles. Some of the Upper School children walked round four or more times and were fairly exhausted, but the splendid sum of £1,268.36 was raised and sent to His Royal Highness. Amid all these events and celebrations was the foundation of the Former Pupils' Association, which was to make a significant contribution to the School. Appropriately, Susan Hampshire was elected as the first President – with Ann Aitchison as the Honorary Secretary and Alexandra Wax as Honorary Treasurer. At a ceremony in Hyde Park, Susan planted a tree in commemoration of the Queen's Silver Jubilee and the foundation of the Former Pupils' Association.

During the next five years, the Association called on the services of Emily Aitchison, Fiona Aitken, Kirsty McCombe, Kendall Page, Caroline Segrave, Elwyn Taylor, Rosemary Thomas and Penelope Thomson. In particular, the officers and committee of the Fomer Pupils' Association were responsible for much of the organisation of the 50th Anniversary Ball at the Hyde Park Hotel – but it was its first news bulletin which captured the attention of ex-pupils, current pupils and staff, revealing as it did the wide diversity of accomplishments and achievements of former 'Hampshires'. One can mention only a few here, but even these display the breadth of interests and attainment.

Danielle Tee was enjoying success in the media, appearing regularly on television's 'Omnibus' programme and also performing at the Royal Albert Hall in *The Odyssey*. Louisa Sington was training at the San Francisco Ballet School, while Kendall Page was working for Christie's until returning home to Toronto. Alan Maltby was directing a firm of chartered surveyors. Shamin Khan, having obtained degrees in Arabic and Greek civilisations, was looking to make her name in Kuwait in television. Jane Jameson continued to teach dance in the country and at The Hampshire School. Rose Hockey was a senior nurse in a Bristol hospital. Max Hole was working for the BBC after leaving Kent University, and Timothy Douglas had abandoned engineering studies to become a 'blues' guitarist. Michelle and Siobhan Gallagher were at the Arts Educational school in Tring, where Dorothy Ind had once taught, and Michelle was to play in the television version of Enid Blyton's *The Famous Five*. Sheila Moseley (now Mrs Minet) was a physiotherapist working with handicapped children. Miss Jane's own children were all much involved with further education: after leaving Girton College, Cambridge, Eve was training to be a child and adolescent psychotherapist at the pre-school Psychiatric Day Unit of Great Ormond Street Hospital for Sick Children and at the Tavistock Clinic; her brother Paul, having been President of the Union and captain of both cricket and hockey at Kent University, was completing his last year there. Youngest sister, Jill, was reading music and sociology at Sussex University. There were many former pupils studying at universities in the United Kingdom and abroad. Letters and messages would be received from all over the world – and those who had completed their further education were living as far away as Hungary and the USA, Australia and South Africa, Brazil and New Zealand. The spirit of The Hampshire School had penetrated many areas of the globe.

Back at the School, there were first candidates for the Royal Schools of Music examinations and for the Cecchetti Ballet choreographic competition. Honours were gained in exhibitions of children's art organised by the Royal Academy and competitions held by The Poetry Society. Activity was intense but not allowed to overshadow another very important anniversary. It was now 50 years since that first venture in the drawing-room of Oakgates, and the anniversary was celebrated by a Ball at the Hyde Park Hotel in December 1978. This was a magnificent occasion, with 280 people attending, which raised more than £2,300 to open the Anniversary Educational Trust Fund. That was just the start. The Ball was a triumph of organisation and co-operation – sponsored by the Former

The 50th Anniversary Ball, held at the Hyde Park Hotel in 1978 – seen here enjoying the splendid dinner are Miss Jane, Arthur Rodwell, Margaret Hampshire, General Graeme, Mrs Sheila Colonnette, Lady Warner, Mrs Jean Graeme and Christopher Box-Grainger.

Pupils' Association and the Parents' Association. Led by Susan Hampshire and Miss Jane, with the support of no less than 21 members of both new Associations, it could not fail. Nor did it – thanks to the sterling efforts of Mrs Frances Aitken, Maurice Cowin, Simon de Wardener, Mrs Alison Dixon (née Skemp), Max Hole, Camilla Howard, Peter Jackson, Christina Loder, Kendall Page, Mrs Caroline Pereira, Mrs Leila Proudlove, Mrs Amanda Smallwood (née Stewart), Deborah Tapley, Penelope Thomson, Mrs Gillian Usborne (née Graeme), Lady Warner (née Simone Nangle) and Mrs Jenny Woodley. It was a splendid event.

The Hampshire School 50th Anniversary Educational Trust was set up in early 1979 and registered as a charitable Trust in 1980. The constitution and objectives stated that the Trust existed to provide educational facilities at the Schools for children from any background or walk of life deserving of financial or other assistance in order to continue their education at the Schools and beyond; to award scholarships and prizes each year; to provide grants to alleviate parental hardship brought about by wartime death, incapacity and the unfortunate break-up of families. To meet those objectives, the Trust has raised and donated many thousands of pounds over the years and continues to do so. The sales of this history will, it is hoped, swell the funds and allow much more good work and good causes to be addressed in future.

The first Trustees were Major-General Ian Graeme (Chairman), Jane Box-Grainger, Susan Hampshire, Lady Warner (former pupil Simone Nangle), The Rt. Hon. James Prior (now Lord Prior), with Christopher Box-Grainger as Honorary Administrator. Three of those Trustees remain active to this day, and the good work goes on.

Ian Graeme was Chairman of the Trust from its foundation until his death in 1992. During that period, he hardly ever missed attending the annual concerts, prizegivings or sports days. He presented the Trust's prizes on many occasions – always with a charming speech of encouragement to the children, and thanks to the parents for their support of the work of the Trust. He, too, figures very high indeed in the list of friends of the School. He was a loyal and enthusiastic supporter of the School in every way – where his daughter, Gillian, had been a pupil and his son-in-law, Bertie, had taught for a year.

The demand for places at the School grew to such a level that Miss Jane attempted to purchase the adjoining premises of 64 Ennismore Gardens. Planning permission for an annexe to the School had been granted six years before and, now that the lease of No. 64 had become available, it seemed like the answer to all the dreams of further expansion. But, again, Miss Jane's plans were thwarted, for she was beaten in a 'contract race' by a development company. The search for larger or alternative premises in the Knightsbridge area continued – a number of offers were made for buildings – but all came to nothing.

So Miss Jane and her husband decided to look for a new school elsewhere – in France!

The front elevation and inner courtyard of the new School at Veyrines-de-Domme, fully restored and functioning in 1981.

L'Ecole Hampshire

here were, of course, a number of important reasons for looking towards France – not least of which was that integration with Europe was becoming closer every day. The principal European language taught in the School was French, and Miss Jane felt that it was necessary to re-examine the content of the French syllabus and its practice. She was very much aware that low standards of oral French were accepted in many schools and, indeed, by examiners. The statement often expressed – 'Well, everyone speaks English nowadays, so why bother?' – was still prevalent during the early 1970s.

Miss Jane did bother! Her school was fortunate to employ an excellent teacher of French, Mrs Revell-Smith, who was a French national. She had arrived in England believing that she had a good knowledge of the language, only to discover that her awareness of the vocabulary of the most ordinary objects and everyday phrases was limited. So, with Miss Jane she set about devising a syllabus that would guard against such problems and deficiencies for Hampshire pupils. It was agreed that the 45 minute period of the School timetables were of little or no use in helping to attain this vocabulary – the pupils, rushing from one subject to another, often forgot most of what they had learned in the previous class sessions. Obviously, it was desirable to allocate more time and to give greater exposure to the teaching of French – again, more easily stated than achieved. Other examination subjects demanded so much time, and parents, in general, were not themselves linguists and tended to display the peculiarly insular British attitude to Europe.

At this point, we begin to see the vision of June Hampshire extended by her daughter Miss Jane some ten or more steps onwards. Their view that education should take place within *and* outside formal school lessons was to become very fashionable – but, in earlier years, such theories were considered too advanced. In the 1950s, June Hampshire had sent her pupils to shop at Harrods and to tea-rooms in Beauchamp Place. In the 1970s, Miss Jane expanded the original vision by leaving Knightsbridge to cross the Channel to France during term-time, in order that her pupils could gain experience of another living environment. Both women were undoubtedly ahead of their time, although Miss Jane was required to consider the extra dimension of some form of European Union in the future. Avoiding any of the political arguments for and against such a Union, nevertheless she held strong views that her pupils should learn by experience to understand, respect and trust the peoples of other countries. At the same time, they should behave in a disciplined manner as youthful ambassadors of Great Britain. A move to France would, in her opinion, allow a positive reinforcement of her visionary concept.

The solution to the problem appeared to be to found a 'sister' school somewhere in France. Miss Jane and her husband decided to seek and buy a venue there where all pupils aged eight years and above could spend at least ten days annually and where they could be taught in some depth by qualified French nationals. Miss Jane envisaged a boarding-school programme in which children would work on the French language for three hours each morning, giving special attention to the vocabulary of their environment and the acquisition of correct accents. The singing of songs in French is particularly helpful in the production of good accent. They would assist the *femme de ménage* in household tasks and learn something of cuisine and cooking from a French chef. The afternoons would be spent in visits to places of historic interest, châteaux, markets, farms and leisure facilities in the locality – on occasions joining with French children in entertainments and sports. Everything would be geared to assisting the British children to absorb a lasting knowledge of France and its language, customs, culture and people.

Miss Jane planned for the group visits to France to be made during normal term-time, with the pupils being escorted by their own form teachers. There would be no additional costs to parents for the visits, as these would be seen and accepted as an integral part of school life – the School fee structure in England including all costs for travel, tuition, accommodation and insurance for all of those pupils of eight years and over. Only personal pocket-money would have to be found.

This then was the dream, or plan, on which the scheme would be based – curriculum and objectives to be achieved. What remained was to find a suitable property with an infrastructure which could be the foundation for the plan – as well as the essential administrative work of forming a French company, seeking approval of the French Ministries of Education and Finance and of the many regional and local authorities which form the formidable bureaucracy of school life in France.

Undeterred, Jane and Christopher Box-Grainger began their search for a location for a school, but the immediate difficulty was that Miss Jane could spare so little time from the management of the Schools in London. So they decided to devote their Easter holidays to the search over a period of four years – but, at almost every turn, there was frustration. An affordable property with the right amount of space and services did not seem to exist. From these forays, Miss Jane returned home depressed – but never defeated. Much later, she wrote of the long search:

'We made up our minds to cull every newspaper advertisement we could find published in England and France. We had considered the Dordogne region but felt that communications and travel would be difficult. However, after reading a very small property advertisement in *The Sunday Telegraph* in 1976, we concentrated on that beautiful part of France and decided to respond to the advertisement during the Spring half-term. We knew that the eastern Dordogne was full of history and that there were many places of interest for cultural visits. A school in the Périgord was a possibility.

The weather was appalling when we set out to prospect once again. We headed for Bordeaux and then eastwards to the Périgord Noir to find a tiny commune named Veyrines-de-Domme just four kilometres south of the River Dordogne – where there was an empty farm *domaine* for sale. We were guided along winding and hilly

ABOVE: The entrance to the courtyard with the barn beyond – as first seen by Miss Jane in 1977, completely overgrown by invading briars, nettles and weeds. The original 18th-century wrought-iron gates were rusted but intact.

ABOVE RIGHT: To the left of the courtyard were a derelict bake-house and ruined pig-sty. The courtyard had to be cleared, the termites exterminated and the ground excavated for the laying of essential services ducts.

country roads to arrive in the centre of the village to see a collection of ruined buildings which stood around a courtyard on one side of the central square or *place*. Almost adjoining the ruins was a rather unprepossessing Mairie. As we looked about us, it began to snow! All we could see otherwise were two farms, an ancient church and presbytery, a tall house on a hillside and a rather nice period house occupied by the Mazet family. My heart sank. I believed that this was to be another wasted visit at much expense, and that my ambition of giving our British pupils a real chance to develop their French would never be realised.

I learned that German troops had occupied the village during the last War – guarding some 180 prisoners, slave labourers and deserters from occupied countries. The prisoners lived a dreadful life, working in the lignite mines and limestone mills at the nearby village of Allas and sleeping in the *domaine* buildings. The guards were housed in an adjoining building (now the Mairie) built by the prisoners after normal work, while officers lived in some comfort up the hill at the tiny sub-hamlet of La Raze. We stared at the large farmhouse, barn and outbuildings – the agent telling us that the property we were considering had not been occupied since the end of the War. It was

Where to start? The new proprietors contemplate the far-from-promising scene.

no wonder that the buildings were in such a ruinous state! In front of the main building was a large ash tree riven by lightning, and what appeared to be the village well and wash-place. Round the corner, we found wrought-iron gates to the inner courtyard. If we had anticipated seeing a beautiful group of Périgourdin stone houses full of charm, then we were to be bitterly disappointed. By the gates, was an ancient *four* (oven) with a leaning bake-house chimney; and the courtyard was full of briars, nettles and weeds – chest and head high in places. In one corner was a ruined pig-sty.

The main buildings were genuinely *de la région*. The *mas* was really two buildings which had been joined together at some stage well in the past. The keystones of both the *mas* and *grange* bore the building dates of 1782 and 1790.'

It would be hard to imagine what thoughts went through the minds of the Box-Graingers as they surveyed the dilapidated farm *domaine*. Whatever its state of decay, this property in a rural district of the Dordogne offered sanctuary, and, for Miss Jane, the knowledge that her

The building's two-foot thick stone walls had to be treated, 'dressed' and prepared for new doors and windows.

pupils would be safe was important. This was no sentimental or whimsical fancy, but a necessary consideration. For it must be recalled that in the 1970s the Knightsbridge area had suffered a number of political and terrorist incidents which had affected the Schools. Because of the siege at the Iranian Embassy, the Upper School at Ennismore Gardens had been forced to close for four days. A policewoman had been tragically killed by an IRA bomb very close to St Saviour's Hall – and, from the windows of Ennismore Gardens, one had been able to see a file of Libyans being deported by a squad of London police officers.

These events had underlined the fact that, before taking on a school in France, it was imperative to determine the safety and security of children boarding some 700 miles from their homes in England. This was a major consideration – and the peace and tranquillity of Veyrines-de-Domme was an important factor in Miss Jane's decision to buy the property. However, there are many other things to face and take into account. Miss Jane remarks:

'While my husband and I accepted that the site had great potential, although lacking any supplementary land area, we could not ignore the fact that there would be a daunting volume of work and associated cost in developing the existing building "shells" into an operational school. The original stone walls and general architecture were full of promise – but there would be massive expense in installing modern

The *grange* had originally been roofed with layers of *lauze* – handcrafted limestone tile slabs – now mostly fallen in to the earth floor.

systems of sewage, water supply, electricity, gas, fire alarm and safety equipment. there would have to be new roofing, new doors and window-frames, new flooring, heating systems – and, obviously, there would be further cost in procuring new furniture and other internal equipment.

In spite of the volume of work and cost which lay ahead, we decided to purchase the site on the spot. Leaving behind a somewhat bewildered agent, we went off to enjoy a wonderful Périgourdin meal before making our way back to Bordeaux and London. We left France that evening in a fairly euphoric state! At last The Hampshire School would become the first English preparatory school to have its own French branch school, and I would be able to implement my dream of giving my pupils a really sound basis in a European language to prepare them for a future in an ever-shrinking world. I would become the first director (*Gérante*) of a French school company – even though I was English, and a woman at that!'

The purchase of the site at Veyrines-de-Domme was completed in 1977, with L'Ecole Hampshire, SARL (Société à Responsabilité Limitée) being registered as a limited company and subsidiary of Hampshire Tutorials Limited, the service company operating Ennismore Gardens and St Saviour's Hall. But it was not all 'plain sailing' in any respect. A vast amount of legal and administrative work was still to be done. Lawyers, notaries, accountants and consultants based in Paris, Bordeaux and Sarlat strove (at astonishingly high fees) to pilot the enterprise through the treacherous waters of French administrations. Eventually the Ministries of Education and Finance, the authorities for employment and social security, the Département de la Dordogne, Pensions Boards, the Direction Générale des Impôts, the local Registre du Commerce, and seemingly endless other bodies *all* approved L'Ecole Hampshire and its directors as being legitimate. But this was achieved only after sundry officials and legal representatives had sworn affidavits that Madame Jane Box-Grainger was a fit and proper person to care for children and conduct the enterprise under the moral laws of France!

It had taken the best part of two years to complete the whole business but, in 1978, L'Ecole Hampshire, with Miss Jane as *Gérante*, became recognised as legal and acceptable. But even then, the Mayor of the little commune (with only about 200 voting adults) had to countersign various documents giving his overriding approval. Only then could the real work begin and, for some two years, Miss Jane and her husband were engaged in many major tasks. The two principal buildings were protected as places of historic interest with conservation orders, and it was necessary for the renovation and new work to be supervised and approved by the Bureau de Beaux Arts at Périgueux. As it transpired, this group of officials proved to be invaluable in helping to restore the buildings to very nearly their original appearance and by advising on crafts and materials.

Miss Jane says:

'We employed an Anglo-French architect, Johnny Devas, who operated from a small town in the Lot-Quercy region. By chance, he was a cousin of a family of three children who had attended The Hampshire School in the middle of the 1950s. He worked from a place some two hours' drive to the south of our village, and he found it very difficult to attract and commission local *entrepreneurs* although he did a splendid job in obtaining all the necessary and essential planning and building licences.

There were further complications in that, at that time, all craftsmen regarded themselves as individual specialists. At one stage, we found that we were employing no less than seventeen different *entrepreneurs*!'

The year is now 1981 and the School is open and ready to accept pupils.

The Box-Graingers' problems were multiplied by the fact that they had to engage utility services contractors. Electricité de France (EDF) were needed to provide three-phase mains power to a sub-station, and Sogedo SA for a large-bore water supply. From Toulouse came Service Oxyvor for the installation of a sewage and water purification plant, and Télécom France had to provide telephone and fax lines. Then there were suppliers of fire alarm and security systems, PBX telephones, television and video, and – it seemed a never-ending list. It was an immense task, and it needed local help and understanding to make it all possible.

'We were fortunate to gain the expert services of a maître d'oeuvre from the nearby village of Marnac. Bernard Devaux was very experienced

in the restoration of ancient buildings and I don't think we would have succeeded without his knowledge, skills and local contacts. Even with his help, it was still necessary for us to make many visits from London in order to arrange progress payments and to sign various documents.

Almost every weekend, we were concerned with the buying and fitting of kitchen, shower, toilet or electrical equipment. And then there were beds, desks, tables, chairs, curtains, mirrors, audio language laboratory sets and the dozens of other items that are required to establish a boarding school for some 40 pupils and staff.'

By the spring of 1980, L'Ecole Hampshire was open and ready to accept pupils from its parent school in Knightsbridge and from other preparatory schools. A dream had been realised, but Miss Jane trod cautiously and thoughtfully. She recalls:

One of the dormitories on the floor above the *salle de classe.*

LEFT: The ground floor of the *grange* now a large and airy *salle de classe*. Madame Odette Jardin with pupils, including Katie Davies, Frances Graham, Sylvie Mazet, Iona and Tara McCorquodale, Gilles Monod, Ashleigh Seagar, Jennifer Soreck.

BELOW: The *grange* at night.

'I felt it would be wise to run a "pilot course" in order to test out the facilities so, in July 1980, we organised a group made up of the children of friends, some school parents and a few local children. It was even more successful than I could have hoped, notwithstanding the somewhat spartan surroundings. We pressed on to open the school fully in May 1981. It

was the culmination of nearly four years of very hard and very expensive work, but I have never regretted a minute of it, nor a penny of it. It has been thoroughly worthwhile, and I have always been glad that we settled on Veyrines-de-Domme in the heart of the Dordogne.'

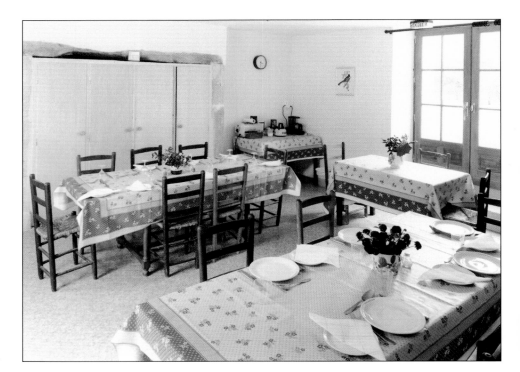

The ground floor of the *mas* (main building) now provides for two dining-rooms, a store room, a cloakroom and a spacious main kitchen. Shown here is one of the dining-rooms.

The glorious Dordogne weather soon persuades all concerned that meals *en plein air* are to be enjoyed.

Miss Jane could well be pleased and proud of her achievement. Within the first decade of the School's existence, more than 3,000 pupils between the ages of eight and 18 from Great Britain, France, Spain, Portugal and elsewhere attended courses at L'Ecole Hampshire. Organised school groups enjoyed and benefited from visits to the French branch. From London came

ABOVE: Georges Pestourie (chef) and Colette Mazet (*femme de service*) cutting a birthday cake for one of the Kensington Gardens pupils.

pupils of Cameron House, Garden House, Falkner House and Lady Eden's schools – from Hampshire pupils of Bedales Junior School – from Hertfordshire pupils of Northfield School – from Surrey the pupils of Hall Grove and Reigate St Mary's schools – from Sussex the pupils of Arundale and Broadwater Manor schools – from Spain a first

LEFT: By 1983 an English garden scene has been created in the courtyard.

LEFT: The once sleepy hamlet of Veyrines-de-Domme has become a busy scholastic scene by 1983, and the School is now rated as the second largest employer in the commune.

BELOW: Miss Eloise escorts a school group to L'Ecole Hampshire in 1986, including Alexandra Aitken, Georgiana Aitken, Dana Al Kotubi, Katherine Bray, Bettina Davidson, Hema Kotecha, Rose Lambert, Catherine Reiffen, Lara Stoby, Frederica West.

group of pupils studying at St Edwin's School in Spain – and finally, the continuing groups from Downe House School in Berkshire. The Hampshire School in Knightsbridge was always given the top priority in the reservation of course dates, even though that privilege did occasionally cause other school groups to postpone or cancel their visits. The School attracted the notice of the press and it has been featured in the pages of *The Times, The Daily Telegraph*, the *Independent, Wall Street Journal, Le Monde, Vocable* and a host of other newspapers. It is a recognised force in Franco-British educational circles.

Whatever the views of the press, or the enthusiasms of Radio Périgord, the ultimate verdict must rest with the pupils. Fiona McOran-Campbell was eleven when she made her first trip to L'Ecole Hampshire. She wrote in the School magazine:

'We had a marvellous time there from the moment we got up to when we went to bed. Quand nous allons en France nous sommes très

Group after group of children attend L'Ecole Hampshire from Britain, Ireland and France, joined by pupils from elsewhere in Europe – Spain, Portugal, Italy, Belgium, Germany – and as far afield as Kenya, Madagascar, Mexico, Trinidad, Canada and the USA. The pupils all live, work and play together in harmony and safety – learning during the mornings and then enjoying swimming, riding, canoeing and cultural visits during the afternoons.

heureuses. Nous avons trois cours par jour. Pendant les leçons nous travaillons avec livre appelé *Eclair*. Le Samedi nous allons au marché à Sarlat et nous achetons des cadeaux. Cette fois nous avons visité les Grottes de Domme, c'était très interessant. Nous avons regardé les stalactites et les stalagmites et nous avons regardé aussi très jolie rivière. Le dimanche nous avons joué au mini golf mais nous avons du marcher pendant huit kilometres. Nous aimons beaucoup y aller. Le soleil brille toujours à L'Ecole Hampshire en France.'

There are some inaccuracies, and there may have been some aid with the French, but there is a glow of happy learning here.

Stasha Palos, a year younger than Fiona, began her article in the magazine with an uninhibited statement – 'I loved France'. And this was echoed by Tala Hadid, who said 'the food was excellent, and everyone was happy'.

When the Box-Graingers answered the advertisement in *The Sunday Telegraph*, they found a mini-paradise. Veyrines-de-Domme is too small a

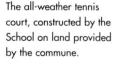

The all-weather tennis court, constructed by the School on land provided by the commune.

Miss Jane stands before her cottage in the courtyard next to a magnificent magnolia tree. This plant was brought to France from London in a pot in 1986, when it was but 20 inches tall. It now stands more than 25 feet high!

village to have a shop, and the School takes up a full side of the central *place*. For shopping, one must go to St Cyprien or Sarlat, ten to 18 kilometres distant, for the markets and cafés, or to Domme, an old *bastide* which looks down on the glory of the magnificent countryside below. This is a fertile area, once ruled by the English for some 300 years, breathtaking in its beauty and almost totally unspoiled. It is noted for its wine, walnuts and chestnuts, mushrooms, and for delicacies like *foie gras* and truffles. The charm of the local architecture and stonework, the blue of the sky and brilliant light, the lush countryside, the total ambience of the eastern Dordogne give a hint of magic which makes all dreams seem possible.

To state that Miss Jane was dazzled by the environment in the Dordogne would not be too much of an overstatement. She recognised that environment plays an important part in the development of children's education and, in particular, their desire to learn more of a new and exciting world.

Thus the instruction at L'Ecole Hampshire is living and vital, with the aim to achieve fluency and confident communication in French within a short time. Miss Jane has never lost sight of what she calls a 'shrinking world'. She insists that her teachers are well aware of the demands of British examinations, but is convinced that a well-planned syllabus meets those demands in full, with the added advantage of happy social contact with local people.

But life is full of change and, in 1993, Miss Jane was persuaded to lease L'Ecole Hampshire on an exclusive ten-year basis to Downe House School – the girls' public school situated near Newbury in Berkshire. Her French teaching and domestic staff are retained by the new occupants to look after some 25 or more girls of the 12 to 13 age-group for three full terms each year – under the supervision of a house mistress from Downe House. Miss Jane is very happy that her pioneering concept has been carried forward by such a prestigious school.

Le soleil brille toujours à L'Ecole Hampshire en France!

Natalie Alwan, aged 11.

Fully Rounded People

ur attention has been focused necessarily on the establishment of the school in France but, in spite of the energy and expense invested in setting up L'Ecole Hampshire, life at the schools in Knightsbridge flowed on with uninterrupted vigour.

Mrs Mavis McCree was appointed Deputy Headmistress in 1979 and, 17 years later, is still teaching English and literature. As already noted, 1979 was the year The Hampshire School 50th Anniversary Education Trust was founded, and the work of the

The staff of the Upper School in 1981 – Miss Fiona, Miss Sarah, Miss Carolyn, Mrs Marie Ince, Miss Mary, Miss Deborah, Mrs E. Smith, Lady Lisle, Mrs Jane Box-Grainger, Mrs Mavis McCree, Miss Doreen and Miss Alice.

Form IVA of the Upper School in 1981 – Mrs Mavis McCree with Suzy Adams, Rana Al Atia, Preeti Farooki, Paola Luce, Charlotte Mallinson, Katherine Miller, Susan Modjahedi, Louise Noel, Dyala Sabbagh, Alice Todhunter.

Trust cannot be overpraised. Most of that work and the benefits arising have been directed to The Hampshire Schools in London. Six academic, music and art scholarships have been awarded annually, as well as 16 form prizes. The Trust has also funded eight scholarships to L'Ecole Hampshire and two to Roedean School. It should be pointed out that the pupils and staff have been responsible for raising much money for the Trust, and that it is their efforts which have helped to make possible the various scholarships, prizes and grants. The most popular methods of raising money were from sponsored walks, swimming competitions and 'spelling bees' – and the proceeds from sales at the School's autumn and Christmas fairs. Before the children became directly involved, the Trust had relied on the generous donations, gifts and covenants from many parents, friends and former pupils. These sums were invested shrewdly and, together with interest from bank deposits, the core funds of the Trust built up to an impressive total.

The Trust depends very much upon the interest and support of the Former Pupils' Association in recording the whereabouts and achievements of its members all over the world: by no means an easy task for the secretaries who followed Ann Aitchison – Kirsty McCombe described it as being more demanding than studying for a degree! But the news of former pupils did reveal a consistent pattern of outstanding success in higher education, achievement in professions and business, and the 'Hampshire' dictum of care and concern for others.

The one activity in which the former pupils appeared unable to excel, was to beat the School at rounders! Kathy Griswold was rather proud of the School's superiority over these 'older' ladies. She said in the School magazine: 'Some of them could hit the ball very far, and run fast. We played in Hyde Park near Rotten Row, and the grass was rather muddy. They batted first and each player had three chances, but they only scored one rounder – we got many people out in the field. When we batted, we won by several rounders.' Inevitably, the game ended with 'a delicious tea of cakes, orange juice, jellies, biscuits and ice cream'!

One of the former pupils, Rosamond Wynn-Pope, had become a functions organiser for the Save The Children Fund – and, after one sponsored walk in Hyde Park, she set up stalls to sell gifts on behalf of the Fund, while the Parents' Association, ever supportive, provided the tea. Mindful of her old school, Rosamond invited 30 of the seven- and eight-year-old pupils to sing in the carol concert staged at the Royal Albert Hall by the Fund. They sang with the Goldsmith's Choral Union, and the concert was televised and shown on BBC 2. Afterwards, the children shook hands with the then Prime Minister, Margaret Thatcher, who autographed their programmes as she made her exit from the Hall.

Perhaps it is time to consider how the School so consistently managed to ally academic success with social awareness. Such alliances do not happen by chance. Miss Jane always believed that education should be innovative, stimulating and enjoyable, and that it should take place in an environment which encouraged learning and avoided boredom. Her breadth of curriculum has given children the opportunity to develop individual talents as fully as possible. The instruction in the arts has been supplemented by a warm encouragement for them to study the history and evolution of their environment – and shown by many visits to museums, galleries, exhibitions and farms. The reactions of the junior pupils illustrate their keen interest and enjoyment.

Alexandra Sherman, aged 6.

Alexandra Lewis (age 5) wrote: 'On Thursday we went to the Natural History Museum, and I liked the Diplodocus and couldn't believe my eyes.'

Pippa Milton (age 6) wrote: 'On Friday we went to Mellow Farm. First we went to the top of a hill for the farmer to show us how long the farm was, and then he showed us how the milking machines worked. Later we found a rabbit.

Sherine Shaker, aged 10.

Margit Ritz (age 6) wrote: 'I liked the Science Museum. I liked the moon and the fire engine and the children's gallery. Miss Alice gave me an electric shock, and I saw myself on television.'

Linnet Taylor (age 6) was rather more down-to-earth when she wrote: 'I went to Mellow Farm and I fell in a cow pat. We saw the cows being milked, and we had lunch in a field.'

Penelope Aitken (age 5) wrote: 'On Thursday IIB went to the Natural History Museum, and we saw the Dinosaurs. We saw Tyrannosaurus Rex, and we saw the Iguanodon. We saw butterflies and insects, then we saw how we were born. I liked the butterflies best. It was fun.'

Lindsay Amon, aged 7.

Michael Mackay-Lewis (age 6) wrote: 'I liked the British Museum. There

Penelope Aitken, aged 5.

were many Roman things. Things of good Romans and bad Romans. The Roman things were very good and very old. All of the British Museum was good.'

The pupils have been taught to have a keen interest in people and in everything going on around them. In short, they are led towards becoming fully rounded people. This is an aim which 'oft was thought' at many educational establishments 'but ne'er so well expressed' as at The Hampshire School.

What was once innovative became an integral part of life at the School – so that pupils competing in the Mabel Ryan Ballet Awards, the gymnastic and dance demonstrations, the inter-house netball matches and the 'Katy Charles' Public

ABOVE: A Nativity play – Miss Jane rehearses five nervous 'angels'.

LEFT: Ten more aspiring 'angels'.

The 1979 concert and prizegiving at the Dorchester Hotel in Park Lane – Susan Hampshire presents prizes to Rebecca Mitchell and Rebecca du Pont de Bie, while Miss Jane stands in the background.

Reading Competition – all introduced in the 1970s and 1980s – were later taken for granted – as became the case with the annual concert and prizegiving, first held at the Dorchester Hotel in Park Lane as far back as 1958. The function was held at the Dorchester for 26 years in succession, and attendances of some 600 parents and children were quite common. The concerts always included dancing (ballet and national), a full-length play or musical such as *The Little Princess, Toad of Toad Hall, The Wizard of Oz, The Snow Queen* and *Joseph and the Amazing Technicolour Dreamcoat.*

A child's simple recollection of a typical concert was written by Amely Greeven (age 9):

'We all went to the Dorchester for our Prizegiving Day. I was going to do a ballet with Anoushka Menzies. When I got in I found Mrs Ind, our ballet teacher, and she told us to change. I was very nervous and could hear the seats filling up with parents and friends. I heard every-one go silent and I peeped through the curtains to see IIIA do their play. Then the ballet began and soon our turn came. Anoushka and I went out to the centre of the Ballroom feeling very nervous. But I was

Pupils enjoying the tea after the concert on Prizegiving Day.

not nervous when I got started. I saw my mother watching and soon heard the last notes die away – I felt quite triumphant. I hurried back to change for the play and changed just in time! I was in the chorus of *Joseph and the Amazing Technicolour Dreamcoat*, with Iona McCorquodale as Joseph, and it went off very well. After a break we had a delicious tea (the best part of the Prizegiving Day) and we ate as much as we could. Then we were ready for the Prizes. I had won the senior Good Work Cup and the Form prize, and was runner-up for a ballet cup. It was an exciting day and I was very tired when it was all over.'

But, excitement apart, the prizegiving incurred a great deal of hard work for Miss Jane. Standing behind a long table laden with silver cups and trophies, prizes and certificates, she had to make a speech listing the events of the academic year, introduce the distinguished guest and announce as many as 60 names of winners. Over the years, the prizes have been presented by many distinguished people – including the Reverend Francis Anderson, The Lady Catto, Miss Rhoda Colville, General

Graeme, Susan Hampshire (now Lady Kulukundis), Mrs Ann Longley, Dame Pattie Menzies, Lady Monson, Lady Pierson Dixon, Hon. Mrs R. G. Phillimore, Baroness Pike, Lady Prior, Princess Rigamonti Tasca di Cuto and Lady Rowan.

At the School itself, the people of tomorrow thrived. Mrs Ann Sharp (Miss Ann) returned to the Lower School in 1974, and became its Head in 1980. She followed Miss Philippa after her six years in the Hall. Although Mrs Sharp was a successful Head, it became necessary for her to undergo hip-replacement operations and she was forced to retire again after only four years. Parents were very sorry to see her leave, since she was recognised as the best teacher of reading in London. However, she has continued to teach the piano and her results have always been outstanding. One of her young pupils wrote:

'I am in the music group, it is fun. We did a concert on Wednesday. The day of the concert was very exciting, and the mummys and daddys came to see us. Our music teacher is Mrs Sharp and she was very nice and I liked her very much. We had a song with instruments that was fun as well and Omar was the conductor. When the concert was over the mummys and daddys gave us a big cheer and then we had some tea. We had a drink of orange juice and biscuits and then we went home.'

From 1982 to 1986, Hampshire School pupils achieved some quite remarkable academic results. Gabrielle Darbyshire won an open scholarship to Roedean, followed later by Linnet Taylor. Louise Noel became the first pupil to win an open scholarship to Sherborne School for Girls, and she was followed by Samantha Wilson. Catherine Peppiatt won the first exhibition and foundation scholarship to Queen Anne's School, Caversham, followed by Leanda Reed with a music exhibition. Lena Sentongo won a scholarship to The Ladies' College, Cheltenham – where Miss Jane's cousin, Margaret Hampshire, had once been Principal. Then James Grant Peterkin won the Top Scholarship to St Aubyn's School, and no less than 128 other places to the public schools of their first choice were won by the School's Common Entrance candidates. A 'golden' period for the School!

Mrs Carolyn Pringle, form mistress of IIIB, started a poetry club as an after-school activity. The response from pupils was typically enthusiastic, to the point that 25 children were entered for the spring public examinations of The Poetry Society. The results were excellent – all 25 gaining honours, credits and passes. Mrs Pringle wrote: 'The children enjoyed reciting the poems aloud and I hope that the interest will continue.'

One of the strengths of the School was that such interests were never simply inward-looking. There was no element of selfishness or jealousy, and the accomplishment of others was always applauded. An example of this occurred when the School recognised the contribution to its life for a quarter of a century by the Vicar of St Saviour's Church, the Reverend Francis Anderson. The School had had strong links with St Saviour's and donated gifts regularly to the November fairs held by the church. In one year alone, the church benefited by £2,374 from items contributed by the parents and pupils. An 11 year-old, Olivia Campbell, was entrusted with the task of presenting the Vicar with a gift cheque for his conduct of the School's church services for 25 years. Olivia was to write:

Richard Du Cann QC, Mrs Marley Du Cann and the Rev. Francis Anderson at the 50th Anniversary Ball.

'After the service on Monday morning, I waited until everyone was quiet and then I walked up to Mr Anderson and said, "We are grateful to you for letting us use your church every Monday, and the Hall. We felt that as you have been running the church for so long that we would like to present you with a small gift, and we hope that you will accept it from all children of The Hampshire School – thank you very much." The Vicar thanked us very much, and hoped that we had learned something from his talks to us over the years. He also said that he had enjoyed meeting generations of "Hampshire" children. Then we all filed out of the church and went back to school.'

In 1985, 57 years after foundation, the School received the 'official' recognition it had so long deserved. It underwent a three-day period of inspection and monitoring by the Department of Education and Science and the Independent Schools Joint Council (ISJC) – and those who have not been subject to such a process cannot imagine what is involved.

Before the inspectors arrived at the School, they called for copies of the following:

- the School prospectus
- the schedule of fees for the academic year
- the School magazine
- the list of teachers by name and qualifications
- the list of ancillary staff
- form lists of pupils with their ages
- the prospectus for L'Ecole Hampshire
- the facilities and venues for sport and recreation used
- the timetables and annual programmes
- the School date lists
- the syllabus
- the School hymn book (printed by the Trust).

After a thorough inspection of the buildings at Ennismore Gardens and St Saviour's Hall – paying special attention to the state of cloakrooms and lavatories, the fire escapes and safety equipment, the kitchen and quality of the lunches – they turned their attention to an inspection of the teaching and quality of teaching staff, who were asked to explain the books used, the exercises and the items written on blackboards. Lists of equipment were demanded and the use of that equipment was queried.

The science laboratory and library were also inspected and details of regular use were required. Discipline, the mood of the children, the drawings on the walls, the numbers in each class, the schemes for homework – all came under scrutiny. Also the relationships between staff and pupils, between the Head and staff and between individual members of staff, were studied – everything was monitored in detail. For those being examined, it was a taxing experience.

The result of this comprehensive inspection of The Hampshire School was that it was commended at the highest level of excellence in regard to efficiency, academic standards and the welfare of its pupils. The School was granted full accreditation.

Miss Jane's repeated dictum that the priority of any school is to produce fully rounded people for service to all in later life, has already been illustrated in this history. Taken at random, and in addition to those former pupils already mentioned, there are a number of names which should be noted: Belita Jepson–Turner became a champion ice-skater and dancer, Britain's answer to Sonja Henie; Helen Noble (Mrs Penney), a former pupil who sent her three children to the School before returning to Ireland; Susan Hampshire (now Lady Kulukundis), who received four Honorary Doctorates in literature, education and arts from universities in the City of London, Kingston, St Andrews and Boston; Colette Keen from Australia, winner of theatre and script awards for her artistic work in Australia and California; Caroline Steel for her important work as a physiotherapist; Alexander Ward-Jackson who presented very interesting programmes on art and museums on BBC television.

It was always a pleasure to receive news of past pupils, and the link of the past to the present has been a constant source of refreshment. From Roedean, Gabrielle Darbyshire went up to Cambridge, and graduated in science. Her sister, Alexandra (Alex), graduated from Durham University with triple honours in four languages. However, both graduates opted for a career in law with much success. There were four Du Cann children at the School, all of whom maintained contact. Charlotte then worked on the 'Shop Hound' column of *Vogue* and Ruth, after courses in Florence and St Martin's School of Art, became a fashion assistant for *Harpers & Queen*. In 1984, she selected clothes for her mother to wear as part of a

Sunday Express Magazine feature entitled 'How Would Fashion Editors Dress Their Mums?' Ruth dressed her mother well, just as she did several pupils of The Hampshire School whom she had selected to model in a London fashion show at the Park Lane Hotel. She now lives in Hong Kong as editor of the Far Eastern edition of *Elle*. Charlotte went on to write features and books on fashion and travel, and became the leading writer on fashion for the *Independent*. Christian Du Cann followed in his father's footsteps in becoming a barrister-at-law. He also became the father of twin sons and, according to certain journalists, 'one of the sharpest dressers around'!

Other former 'Hampshires' were also seen to have done well. Lois Cowin was appointed senior orthoptist at Basingstoke District and Lord Treloar Hospitals in Hampshire; Anthony Elliot had founded the very successful *Time Out* magazine group, which he directs to this day; Jeannie Fritts was researching African art at the Smithsonian Institute in Washington; Arminé Guzelian had become the owner of The Busy Bee Nursery School; Susan Hampshire had been honoured with an OBE for her services to the Dyslexia Institute; Samantha Hack was teaching at Oakhill Preparatory School, Dulwich; Peter Hartnell was running his own company trading in precious metals; Yolande Kemp was an administrator and auctioneer for a fine arts company; Conrad McDonnell had won the gold medal for Great Britain at the International Olympiad for Students in Austria – his winning subject being physics; Andrew Morgan had become manager of the Spanish branch of the Coats Paton Textiles Group; Sherine Shaker was working in Paris at the headquarters of UNESCO; Thomas Ind had qualified as a doctor; Louella Garrick had gained critical acclaim as an artist; successful businessman, Paul Zaphiriou, had entered his daughter Alexandra in the Lower School; Anne Parmiter was a former pupil who then came back to teach at the School for a number of years, and then went on to other schools; Fenella Rosenwald (mother of Celia) taught at the School and then became the secretary of the Former Pupils' Association before retiring to Oxfordshire; Amanda Howard taught in the Kindergarten, after which her two children, Sophie and Michael, attended the School before the family left to live in Spain.

The young people moving on from The Hampshire School to higher education and beyond could take inspiration and comfort from the achievements of those who had gone before them. Like Alexander the Great, who may have run out of worlds to conquer, of the pupils and former pupils of the School it could be said that 'every morning brought a noble chance'.

The range of occupations, interests and study was astonishing. It included accountants, actresses, architects, army officers, artists, auctioneers, authors, bankers, biochemists, consultants, dancers, diplomats, doctors, editors, experts in many fields, explorers, fashion designers, horticulturalists, hospital specialists, journalists, lawyers, musicians, owners of galleries and other businesses, painters, professors, restaurateurs, teachers, therapists, yachtsmen, welfare workers and much more. There are former 'Hampshires' on every continent. None of them can ever measure the debt they owe to those formative years in Knightsbridge, or to the brilliant Miss Jane and her dedicated teams.

Miss Jane always considered it to be an important compliment and recommendation when whole family groups applied to attend the School. Reviewing the pupil registers after so many years, she was happy to recall the very many such groups who had come under her care in London and France. Perhaps it is not surprising that a school of such distinctive character, direction and activities should attract many parents from all walks of life. The obvious calibre of the teachers, visiting staff and examiners became widely known, and the geographical situation of the School was another attraction. Knightsbridge and the surrounding area was in the so-called 'embassy belt', alive with famous shops and restaurants, and almost a magnet for people striving to recover from five years of wartime privation.

The School has always attracted pupils of many nationalities. It has to be appreciated that pupils from overseas have made a great contribution to the School. The pupils have been fortunate to have friends of different cultures which has made it easier for them to integrate in the ever-shrinking world.

St Saviour's Hall and, later, Ennismore Gardens rang with the enthusiastic voices of large families and their friends. Several of these family

Some more guests at the 50th Anniversary Ball – Miss Victoria Aitchison, Sir Nigel and Lady Broackes and Miss Ann Aitchison.

names have appeared in the foregoing pages – Aitkens, Aitchisons, Broggers, Darbyshires, Du Canns, Hendersons, McDonnells, Phibbs, Russells, Skemps and Steels, to name but a few. Unfortunately, not all former pupils can now be traced, but all available avenues of enquiry have been followed in an attempt to produce a roll of pupils attending the

School from 1928 to the end of the 1980s (Appendix A, pp. 117–131). For reasons of time and space, it has regrettably not been possible to include all of those who attended the former London Ballet School and L'Ecole Hampshire in France, nor indeed the hundreds of young people who gathered happily at the holiday ballroom classes in London.

The roll of pupils appearing at the end of this book is the best that can be achieved to date. Miss Jane hopes that the circulation of this book will attract readers to forward more information on names and addresses – which, all being well, can be included in a second edition.

All too rarely are schools given the praise that is their due. A school is not just bricks, mortar, desks and chairs – it is a living entity whose well-being and personality is dependent upon those within it. Our lives are shaped by whom we meet and with whom we come into contact – thus, although promotion and marriage mean that changes in staff are inevitable, it is proper that we try to include some of the teachers who have made lasting impressions on hundreds of children. Former pupils will remember the excellent teachers listed in Appendix B (pp. 132–133). They will also recall many valued members of the administrative and domestic staff, without whom the Schools would not have been able to operate so successfully.

But one of the most 'fully rounded' must be Miss Jane herself – a glowing example to her pupils. In a fruitful life so far she has been a dancer and actress, student of French and Spanish, teacher, headmistress, founder of the School at Ennismore Gardens and L'Ecole Hampshire, author of a series of arithmetical textbooks entitled *Number Patterns*, a loving wife and mother – and now a youthful-looking grandmother. During her long career in education, more than 5,000 children have enjoyed her care in London and France. It is safe to predict that none of them will ever forget her. Very attractive in looks and personality, lively and good-humoured but capable of applying impressive discipline when needed, she has been (and still is) a rôle model for girls and young women.

No matter how happy and successful the School was, times were changing, with more and more pressures having to be borne. Miss Jane felt that the time had come for her to step down from some of her responsibilities. She says:

'My children, and my sister's children, were grown up and pursuing their own successful careers. They were not interested in taking over the School and, rather unhappily, I started to look around for a suitable person or company to succeed me. After 37 years of close association with the School in all its various stages of progress, I felt that I could no longer direct two separate school bodies nearly 700 miles apart. I needed some respite from the heavy burden of management, and I decided to sell The Hampshire School and the property in London.'

In 1984, Miss Jane had been approached by Mr Kevin McNeany, chairman of Nord Anglia Education PLC, regarding possible purchase of the School. His Nord Anglia Education Group appeared to be an ideal organisation to take over the School. It already owned and managed preparatory and senior schools in the country and was the largest company providing private education in Britain. Since 1994, it also supplied other educational services such as a schools inspection service under contract to the government's Office for Standards in Education (OFSTED). The Group wished to expand into the London area and, after discussions, it was agreed that the School could be purchased by Nord Anglia Education PLC sometime in the future.

However, as the ISJC accreditation procedures had been set in motion for 1985, Miss Jane wanted to defer the sale until that phase of development had been completed – when she felt she could hand over the reins without complication. It was agreed that Miss Jane would find and appoint a suitable new Head.

As has been seen, the programme of accreditation was accomplished smoothly and successfully, and it soon became time to seek a replacement for Miss Jane. An advertisement in the *Times Educational Supplement* produced about sixty applications, of which ten were short-listed for interviews. Among them was a young man, Arthur Bray, a graduate of South Devon Technical College and Redland College, Bristol University. He was then senior housemaster of Edgarley Hall, the junior branch of Millfield School, with some ten years of responsibility for nearly 250 boarders. Incidentally, he had also had charge of four brothers of former Hampshire School pupils – David and Michael El Hadj, Brett Palos and

Form IVB of the Upper School in 1981 – Mrs Marie Ince with Alexandra Aitken, Henrietta Bevan, Tina Cantwell, Caroline Church, Gay Darbyshire, Rowan Douglas, Charlotte English, Kiron Farooki, Sarah Griswold, Randa Kayyali, Fiona McOran Campbell, Heather Monro, Charlotte Moore, Catherine Peppiatt, Daniella Sanger, Hilary Singer, Justine Suissa.

Christoffer Naess. Apart from his experience at Edgarley Hall, there were other factors in his favour – he was very familiar with the requirements of junior pupils, he had two young children of his own, he was alive to parental concerns and his wife was an experienced school secretary. Although the success of a Head can only really be achieved by practice and experience, Arthur Bray showed that he had the qualifications necessary as a basis for future success.

The transfer of ownership of the London schools and staff had included an agreement for the continued attendance of 'Hampshire' pupils at L'Ecole Hampshire for a period of at least four years. But in 1992, The Hampshire School did not make its usual booking. Arthur Bray wrote:

'We were committed to the idea, started by Miss Jane, that Hampshire School children should have the advantage of being able to have annual study visits to L'Ecole Hampshire in France as an integral part of the School's curriculum. However, with the 1992 visits complete and arrangements having been made for Downe House School to attend Veyrines-de-Domme for three terms of the coming year, it left The Hampshire School with three options. It could take the children

Enjoying the Ball: Mr Maurice Tapley, Mr and Mrs Bertie Usborne and Miss Penelope Thomson.

to L'Ecole Hampshire at times which in our view were not really suitable, or use a holiday school nearby which Miss Jane had kindly found, or to look for an alternative establishment for that academic year. Reluctantly it was decided to take the third option and, in 1993, the "Hampshire" children travelled to Ecole des Roches in Normandy for their French studies.'

Miss Jane in her office
at the Upper School.

Arthur Bray expressed his regret that his pupils were not able to attend L'Ecole Hampshire as before, and the hope that they would be able to return in future. That was not to be the case and, for the last three years, they have spent their study visits in Normandy. Naturally, Miss Jane was very disappointed to find that she would no longer be welcoming further generations of 'Hampshire' children to her excellent school in the Dordogne, even though she had allowed a period of 19 weeks in 1993 especially for them. She writes:

'After this disappointment, I felt that my title of Honorary Principal was misleading. It was a rôle I had accepted to assist the period of transfer in 1986 and to help parents, staff and pupils to accept and appreciate the new management. Also I had felt it would be valuable to the School if my name and that of L'Ecole Hampshire was linked with the new ownership. By 1992, I came to realise that this applied no longer. Once again, it was time for a personal change of direction and I retired as Honorary Principal and Chairman of the Former Pupils' Association. I remained as a Trustee of the 50th Anniversary Education Trust, becoming its Chairman after the sad death of General Graeme.

It was saddening to realise that the "Hampshire" pupils would not be able to attend the school in France I had founded for them. But, in all our lives, there comes a time when change becomes not only desirable but necessary – however sad. I have had much admiration for Arthur Bray's progressive programme of improvements to Ennismore Gardens and the newer premises in Queensborough Terrace and Wetherby Place – expanding the pupil roll from about 170 to some 300 children. Wetherby Place replaced the somewhat antiquated facilities available at St Saviour's Hall.

I had been advised, and believed, that it would be increasingly necessary to leave the Hall – but one cannot allow its passing without some sense of regret. During my 27 years as Principal of the two school buildings, I enjoyed visits by many former pupils and they always insisted on seeing the Hall again. They recalled their happiness there and expressed amazement at the size of the place – it appeared to be so small to their more mature eyes. So often I heard the words – "But it seemed absolutely enormous when I was small". I am sure that the standards for which I worked over so many years will be maintained within these splendidly renovated and equipped buildings.'

There are many who find it impossible to think of The Hampshire Schools in London and France without thinking of Miss Jane. For some, she *was* the Schools. Nor have some forgotten the part played by her husband, Christopher, who gave support in every possible way in spite of his own career and diverse interests. There were even occasions when he became a last-minute presenter of prizes at the Dorchester Hotel and, on those occasions, he was dubbed 'Mister Jane'!

There was so much work and effort, so much energy and financial commitment, so much sheer enthusiasm, all devoted to every aspect of the School – was it all worth it? Of that Miss Jane has no doubt, saying:

'I have enjoyed every minute of it all. I had a vision of the schools I would like to create, where every child would be happy to attend and gain a love of learning for its own sake and the knowledge which followed. I wanted to extend my mother's vision of education and preparation for later life much more widely. In the 1960s, I accepted that it was not possible to pursue that vision and associated aims without the acquisition of a suitable and permanent base. So I invested the money I had inherited in the purchase of No. 63 Ennismore Gardens in order to make this permanent base. I must say that my decision to take such action during those years did, quite often, result in a number of personal and family sacrifices – but it was all certainly most worthwhile.

I have been fortunate to employ many wonderfully dedicated and talented teachers and have had the pleasure of teaching so many wonderful pupils, I have made countless friends through my work, and have felt very fulfilled by the second career I chose. I have been lucky to have good health so far and to enjoy the love and support of a wonderful family, children and grandchild. Too many "wonderfuls" perhaps – but that's how I really feel about my life in education. Were all my endeavours worthwhile? Of course they were!

I now look forward to working for the 50th Anniversary Educational Trust in its task of raising more and more money in support of deserving children and causes in all sectors of education. Naturally, and in accordance with the Deed of Trust, The Hampshire Schools will always have first claim on the attention of the Trustees. I am now happy to leave the futures of The Hampshire Schools to Arthur Bray and Nord Anglia Education PLC, and that of L'Ecole Hampshire to Downe House School. The whole future looks full of promise, and I am content that it should be entrusted to such capable hands.'

So, almost inevitably, a remarkable era ended – not in sadness but buoyed up by confidence in the future. That ending was not to go unremarked for, as soon as the news of her retirement became known, Miss Jane started to receive very many telephone calls, letters and other messages of appreciation and affection. Some can be quoted in this book as a fitting memorial of her work over so many years.

Mrs Virginia Darbyshire wrote:

'When my family returned to England after five years in the Lebanon and we moved into central London, I felt very out of touch with inner city life and had no idea where to start with the task of deciding on a school for my two small daughters who had scant experience of England let alone a large city. I visited a number of schools before The Hampshire School and became a little despondent – since the emphasis seemed to lie heavily on academic achievement and I didn't know at that time how academic my daughters would be. Then Miss Jane (Mrs Jane Box-Grainger, but always "Miss Jane" to parents and children) showed me round The Hampshire School and explained the wide range of activities that the School had to offer. Her attitude towards primary education was so refreshing that I had no need to look further. She guided her pupils (and their parents) kindly and imaginatively towards developing what each one was best at, be that scholarship or music or ballet or art and always with the reassurance that each child was different. I look back on my daughters' progress through secondary school and then university with a deep sense of gratitude to Miss Jane for laying the foundations so thoroughly.'

Patricia Greenwood recalled:

'It was a happy school where both teamwork and individuality were allowed to grow. Its strength came from Miss Jane, a revered Headmistress, from whom praise was always forthcoming with discipline strict but fair. The summer prizegiving and concert at the Dorchester Hotel showed all that Miss Jane had instilled in her pupils. I remember the essence of enjoyment of life shown in the play we performed in front of proud parents. But once our faces were free of make-up and costumes were exchanged for white dresses; the deportment, etiquette and consideration for others was apparent as the rest of the afternoon unfolded. Miss Jane was fully involved in our education, and all of us that entered through the doors of 63 Ennismore Gardens have been able to walk on into life with the great advantage of her teaching.'

Sir David and Lady Steel wrote:

'Memories of Miss Jane bring memories of childhood happiness in St Saviour's Hall and Ennismore Gardens for our family. There was always a welcome and a smile when we appeared, always instant interest and encouragement, infinite patience and a sense of fun with a twinkle in her eye – but always there was Miss Jane, the Head, in quiet control. She gave our children and all others lucky enough to come under her care roots for their future education and progress, and a loyal love of The Hampshire School.'

Mrs Nanice Serageldin wrote:

'I have always felt proud and fortunate that my two daughters received their early education at The Hampshire School in Knightsbridge and France. Miss Jane made their stay with her a happy and enriching experience. She knew every pupil as an individual personality and encouraged them to give of their best at all times. She had a strong personality herself, she was broadminded and able to accept without difficulty differences in national cultures and religions, she was very fair in dealing with any grievance but was always notable in having a special bond with her pupils. The academic standard of the School was very high, particularly in regard to French and the arts, and was evident when my daughters went on to secondary school and university where they were described as being very advanced. There is so much to say of Miss Jane, without whom The Hampshire School could never be the same.'

Mrs Elwyn Taylor wrote that, as a former pupil and then parent, a tribute to Miss Jane is long overdue:

'Over the years the gifted young teacher, Jane Hampshire, developed into Jane Box-Grainger, the outstanding Headmistress – but to all pupils and their parents she is, and always will be, "Miss Jane". A unique combination of wisdom, authority and warmth has been the hallmark of her career with The Hampshire Schools. Her counsel and, when necessary, goading (always disarmingly administered) have often been just what was needed at critical times in her pupils' lives. Perhaps only many years later will those of us who once attended the Schools be aware of what Miss Jane's teaching skills and administrative abilities, coupled with seemingly boundless energy, did to transform our lives. If "all the world's a stage", then Miss Jane has helped many of the world's performers in many spheres, but now it is time for her to take a bow. This book should enable us to see her achievement in its true perspective and to give her at least some of the applause which is her due.'

Mrs Anne Thomas took time from a very busy professional life to write what she called 'a few inadequate words' about Miss Jane:

'In our opinion the first few years of any child's life are the most important, and the grounding our three received was outstanding. Miss Jane was certainly a guiding light: totally gifted and dedicated in every respect to their current and further education. At any time, day or night, she knew exactly what stage they were at in any subject and was able to advise any homework or extra reading they should do if some ailment or other prevented them from coming to school. There cannot be many of that "ilk" anywhere now, and there were certainly not then! What a joy to we parents to know that the standards our children reached would, thanks to Miss Jane's care and devotion, enable them to fly into the schools of their ultimate choice.'

Lord Wakehurst wrote: 'Our first meeting with Miss Jane was in the early 1960s, when we were desperate to find a school for our son who was difficult to control and who, we discovered later, was autistic. Miss Jane accepted him and our daughter, and both benefited enormously.

Portrait of Miss Jane by Catherine Davies.

I shall not forget the wonderful atmosphere of the School and the attention of the pupils to learning. Clearly they were inspired. And all this in a church hall which would not be approved today. Thank you Miss Jane'.

All of this recognition of Miss Jane's esteem in the eyes of former pupils and parents is but a small selection from the many letters of praise of her and the School received when this history was announced. We have recorded the past – for the future of The Hampshire Schools, we must now turn to Arthur Bray and Nord Anglia Education PLC.

Erin Wundram, aged 8.

The New Hampshire Schools

The Nord Anglia Education Group was founded more than 15 years ago by its present Chairman, Kevin McNeany. A former lecturer in further education, he founded the Group with the idea of developing educational establishments of excellence in the independent sector. The Group now includes preparatory schools, senior schools and full-time language academies, and has even pioneered the establishment of British-style preparatory and senior schools in Eastern Europe, the former Communist bloc.

Left to right – Mr Arthur Bray, the Lady Mayoress (Mrs Carolyn Mabey), Mrs Diana McGuinness, Mrs Frances Aitken, Mrs Trisha Stewart-Hodges, Mrs Ann Sharp.

The parent company does not impose a stereotyped pattern on its schools. It helps them all to develop their own individual characteristics and personalities, knowing that these are determined by the historical perspective of the school, the area in which it is situated and the staff, pupils and parents.

Nord Anglia Education is concerned with maintaining standards of excellence, and it was the proven excellence of The Hampshire School, in reputation and achievement, which attracted them to purchase it.

Arthur Bray became Head of The Hampshire School in 1986. The son of a farmer, he studied in Bristol, being one of the first to benefit from training in the technological changes and concepts that were revolutionising ideas on education.

He was appointed to a teaching post at Edgarley Hall, Glastonbury, where he became senior housemaster. Edgarley Hall is the junior school of Millfield School, renowned throughout the world, and is a dynamic, forward-looking establishment, thus providing Arthur Bray with a splendid grounding for the atmosphere of electricity and energy that he was going to find in Knightsbridge.

During his time at Edgarley Hall, Arthur Bray took responsibility for many interesting projects. He started holiday courses in English as a foreign language and a multi-activity course catering for up to 200 eight- to 13-year-olds each week. He assisted with the setting up of a special needs unit and was entrusted with a quarter of a million pounds with which to set up an art, craft and design centre. This task was accomplished and, in a period of ten years, he saw Edgarley Hall grow to a school with 243 boarders in seven houses.

His wife, Diana, had been the Headmaster's secretary, the domestic bursar and senior house mother, so that both the Brays were highly experienced in a wide range of school activities before moving to The Hampshire School.

It was in September 1986 that the Nord Anglia Education Group acquired the School, but, as Jane Box-Grainger has said, the transition was effected very smoothly. Nevertheless, a new Head or any new teacher has initial problems.

'I suppose the great problem I had was in following Miss Jane,' says

Arthur Bray. 'She was such a forceful, charismatic character who had brought the School up to the highest level and it made her a very hard act to follow. Thankfully, as Honorary Principal, she was most supportive and helped me through any teething troubles.'

If there were any teething troubles, they were never noticed by the children. The social awareness of the children was as committed and as commendable as ever. The Christmas fair in 1986 raised £1,725.93 which was divided between three charities, Save The Children, Leukaemia Research and Kidney Dialysis.

Emily Pringle not only thrived academically at the age of nine and was awarded a prize by The Hampshire School 50th Anniversary Educational Trust, she also organised a group of her friends to raise money for World Vision in support of water projects throughout the world. Emily had already done the 'famine' once, but, for her second effort, she was accompanied by ten of her classmates. She wrote in the School magazine: 'The idea was to fast for 24 hours without having food. We could drink fluids but not eat. If we managed to do it the people who sponsored you would have to give you the money. We raised £560.88 and saved about 140 lives!'

As soon as school ended for the summer holidays, the renovation of Ennismore Gardens began with the refurbishment of the top three floors to include a new science laboratory and a computer room. This was the first of a series of developments concerning the School.

The second came in 1988 when the School celebrated its 60th anniversary. The occasion was marked by the planting of a row of six lime trees in Exhibition Road, and by planting another six trees (two oak, two ash and two elm) in Hyde Park. More significantly, perhaps, a second London school, The New Hampshire School (Kensington Gardens), was opened in Queensborough Terrace just to the north of Kensington Gardens.

The house in Queensborough Terrace had been used by the National Childbirth Trust, and it consisted of offices and a classroom, but it had once been a school of music so the building had a history with educational connections. Nord Anglia were supportive of Arthur Bray's idea that it was a good site for the further development of the School, and they

Twins Ben and Chris
Wood arriving at The
New Hampshire School
(Kensington Gardens).

were happy to purchase the freehold. There remained the question of applying for planning permission to use the building for educational purposes.

'We were told,' remembers Arthur Bray, 'that it would take eight weeks to get permission. In fact, it took 18 before the application was considered by the Planning Committee and then it was passed in three minutes – the only condition being that a guard rail should be erected on the pavement.'

The delay in obtaining permission meant that the original nine pupils destined for Kensington Gardens School began the winter term in St Saviour's Hall before moving into No. 9 Queensborough Terrace on 4 October 1988. The building was officially opened by the Lady Mayoress of Westminster on Friday 23 June, the following year.

The new Knightsbridge Under School at No. 5 Wetherby Place, replacing St Saviour's Hall in 1993.

Arthur Bray commented in his foreword to the 1988 School magazine that he had 'the pleasure of showing some former pupils around the School as prospective parents. They had fond memories of their time at The Hampshire School and commented that it was the friendly family atmosphere, as well as the excellent preparation for adult life, that (with hindsight) they now appreciate most about the time they spent at the School.'

The plan was that the new School would operate in parallel to Ennismore Gardens. In this respect, the vision was that the Schools would mirror each other. The Knightsbridge system was replicated at the

ABOVE: In the computer laboratory at Ennismore Gardens, Catherine Earnshaw, Julia Graham and Monica Larkin enjoy a lesson in information technology.

RIGHT: The design studio at Kensington Gardens, with Richard Bray, Natalie Castro, Marco Duyanovich, Yusri Johari and Crystal Whitaker working at craft design and associated technology.

Kensington Gardens School in rooms, equipment and style so that a child could move from one school to another without feeling in awe of being in a different place.

There was still ambitious work to be done in Queensborough Terrace, namely the construction of three rear and two upper-floor extensions.

This was an immense task, and the contractors agreed to complete the work in 19 weeks. They began two days before the start of the Christmas holiday period in 1991. Every effort was made to keep school life within the building normal, but builders scurried all over its exterior. The top floor was vacated, Arthur Bray's office was used as a classroom, and a television lounge in a hotel in the next terrace was rented and converted into a classroom to accommodate

ABOVE: Jasmin Kirpalani receives a violin lesson from Miss Claire at The Knightsbridge Under School, Wetherby Place.

LEFT: Future ballerinas? Leyli Bassiri and Sarah Leat at the barre at Ennismore Gardens.

another class. The children were taken to the park by mini-bus in the break, and everybody had lunch at Queensborough Terrace in order to keep the School together as much as possible.

Remarkably, this massive building project was completed before the beginning of the summer term. It provided the Kensington Gardens School with new cloakrooms, a staff room, a library, a laboratory, teaching rooms and external fire escape, as well as an art, craft, design and technology studio.

With work at Queensborough Terrace finished, attention was turned to Ennismore Gardens where the ground floor was extended and completely refurbished.

Both schools mirror each other in design and style. A child is at home in both. Several teachers operate in both buildings, and the two Schools share several joint activities and go on visits together.

Arthur Bray is emphatic that there has been nothing revolutionary in this restructuring. He sees it as an evolutionary process aimed at offering families full educational choice in order to benefit the majority of children. He is deeply sensitive to the history, the excellent reputation and the astonishing successes of The Hampshire School that he inherited, and he is at pains simply to build on those magnificent foundations.

He touched upon the point in his Headmaster's address at the 1993 prizegiving: 'We have been mindful of the School's traditions, and I am heartened when I hear from long-established parents such as Mrs Aitken and Lady Laws that, in their opinion, the established character and ethos of the School remains unchanged.'

At that time, six Aitken young ladies were following fascinating strands in their lives. Alex had graduated from Exeter University and was a trainee manager in Manchester; Georgiana was at Benenden and in the Kent under-14 athletics team; Fiona was a qualified chartered accountant and was with Coopers & Lybrand; Penelope was on her way to Christ Church, Oxford, to read history; Sarah was working for J. P. Morgan Merchant Bankers in New York and was engaged to be married; while Lucinda was running her own amateur operatic society and her own interior design company.

Other former pupils were also continuing to feature in the national

Mr Arthur Bray and Susan Hampshire talk to the Head of French, Mrs Jacline Revell-Smith.

press. Paul Box–Grainger led Old Tonbridgians to victory in the Cricketer Cup, Deborah Tapley was the South-East England Ballroom Dancing Champion, and Susan Hampshire was gracing the stage in *Noël and Gertie*. As Lady Kulukundis, she has never lapsed in her commitment to the School and, on 12 November 1993, she planted an oak tree in Hyde Park to commemorate The Hampshire School's 65th anniversary. Susan was precise and firm in the planting, having confessed that the last tree she had planted in the Park had died.

There was a tinge of sadness to the occasion in that Major-General Ian Graeme had died a few months previously. As Chairman of the Trust and a founder Trustee, he had given unsparingly of his time to the School and he was much missed. His daughter Gillian, herself a former pupil of the School, represented him at the ceremony.

Mrs McCree wrote in the 1992 School magazine:

'We were all sad to hear of the death of General Graeme who has been Chairman of the Hampshire School Educational Trust for many years.

I did not know him well, but was always impressed by his friendliness, especially to the children. At the 1992 Sports Day during the lunch break, I sat next to him on a bench overlooking the Sports field where he had just presented the prizes. As we shared our sandwiches, we chatted together. I noticed that in the last few months since I had last seen him, his health had deteriorated and he seemed somewhat frail, so I wondered if the day's proceedings might not have been too much for him. I said how kind it was that he had been willing to go to the trouble not only to present the prizes at Sports Day but to watch the events. He immediately said it was no trouble and that he thoroughly enjoyed seeing and talking to the children. He later accepted a lift in the school bus and when we set him down at his destination, he departed with a cheery wave.

Rather than mourn his death, we celebrate a full and productive life very much enhanced, I am sure, by his involvement with children and his obvious love for them.'

He was succeeded as Chairman of the Trust by Jane Box-Grainger, who kindly returned to the School in July 1994 to present the Trust's awards at the annual prizegiving. Among the awards were academic scholarships to Daniella Matar and Crystal Whitaker, music scholarships to Leyli Bassiri and Hana Katic, and arts scholarships to Leyli Bassiri and Toby Jones. The presentations included citizenship prizes to Korey Aaronson, Zahirah Abdullah, Lana Anabtawi, Phillip Bueno, Natalie Castro, Georgina Gordon-Smith, Emily Hambi, Anika Kaul, Nazgol Mohtashami, Marina Moradians, Amy St Johnson, Kimia Shedy, James Smith, Marilyn Thompson and Alexandra Willis. Miss Jane's speech was printed in full in the School magazine. In closing, she said:

'I should like to say a few words about the "citizenship" awards. Many years ago, when my mother directed the School, she always made a point of presenting cups and prizes for what she called "deportment" – now considered to be a rather old-fashioned word. When our for-

mer Chairman, General Graeme, initiated the citizenship prizes (now named in memory after his long chairmanship of the Trust), he carried on that tradition in a different form.

I want you all to know how much the Trustees appreciate the continued support of the School, the parents and the children in giving to the funds of the Trust and its work – and thank you all most warmly. The Trustees also admire the manner in which you, Mr Bray, have expanded the Schools so many ways. Thank you again.'

The School magazine had been edited by Mrs McCree since 1987. The magazine had taken a step forward in 1993 with its green cover and revamped lay-out, and the following year it contained a spread of colour photographs for the first time. They showed Arthur Bray, Susan Hampshire and Jane Box-Grainger at the tree-planting ceremony in Hyde Park – and they showed happy children playing football and netball, doing gymnastics and swimming, and engaged in a geography field trip.

An oak tree is planted in Hyde Park in 1983 by Lady Kulukundis (Susan Hampshire) to mark the 65th anniversary of the foundation of the School. Pupils and staff gather for the ceremony and speeches.

The 65th anniversary tree-planting ceremony in Hyde Park – Mrs Diana Bray and Miss Jane chatting to Mrs Gillian Usborne, the daughter of the first chairman of the Educational Trust.

Lady Laws talks to some very young pupils.

There is a refreshing vigour in each of these photographs, and, with Miss Jane looking on proudly at the tree-planting ceremony, there is a reminder of Arthur Bray's words: 'We aim to educate children for tomorrow, not today, but we must never lose sight of the true traditions and values of yesterday.'

A reminder of many people's happy yesterdays disappeared in the summer of 1993 when, inevitably, the School left St Saviour's Hall. Arthur Bray told the story in his prizegiving address a year later:

'The summer holiday was a very busy and exciting time in that we acquired No. 5 Wetherby Place in mid-August and had just two weeks to convert it into a school for young children. Our four factotums

Children in the Kindergarten at Kensington Gardens, including Noor Al Alousi, Eric Chan, Phoebe Mitchell-Innes, Callum Negus-Fancey, Andrew Papadimitriou, Alice Robbins, Olivia Willis.

worked from early morning until very late into the night, getting everything ready, and I do thank them most sincerely for the tremendous amount of extra work they put in at that time.

With that part of the operation complete, the teaching staff had just a couple of days to set up the School. This was done with amazing speed and we were ready to open The Knightsbridge Under School (complete with new brass plaque) on the first day of term.'

There is a delightful serenity about Wetherby Place which makes it admirably suited for the boys and girls between three and six years old for whom it caters. All the children here are prepared for The Knightsbridge Upper School in Ennismore Gardens. It is a building of considerable charm and was originally built for the daughter of William Makepeace Thackeray, the great novelist. It had been used as an educational establishment prior to becoming part of The Hampshire School.

The three buildings are one School under one Headmaster, and Arthur Bray has continued with his policy that the three buildings of the School should replicate each other so that a child may move among them comfortably and easily, without fear or mistrust.

However, it was decided that as the School now consisted of three substantial buildings, it should operate under the title of The Hampshire Schools, and that it should have a new crest and a school motto. Mrs Larkin spent many hours in research and in designing the crest, which is based on the Pavey family crest. Pavey, one will remember, was June Hampshire's maiden name, so that the debt to the founder is indelibly marked.

Mrs McCree devised the motto *Alte Spectemus*, which can be variously translated as 'Let us have lofty aims', 'Let us have high ideals' or 'Let us aspire to the heights'.

As if in confirmation of the motto she had devised, Mrs McCree received a letter from a former pupil, Claire Vallings. Mrs McCree remembered Claire as a rather shy little girl but who, by the time she left and went to Wycombe Abbey, had developed the confidence and maturity that one associated with graduates of The Hampshire School. Now 18, Claire had completed her A-levels, fulfilled an ambition by throwing

After-school activities at Ennismore Gardens – Heba Kabir, Rebecca Laurence, Catherine Reiffen, Suzy Renwick, Soraya Russell and Tala Tayyara enjoy the chess club under the supervision of Mrs M. Varvill.

herself out of an aeroplane for a 2,500 ft parachute drop, and gone with Project Trust as a volunteer to teach English in Brazil.

Claire's bold venture was not unique among former pupils of The Hampshire School. Arthur Bray recalls Anne-Claire Hoyaux, a French girl whose parents settled temporarily in London when they were engaged in work concerned with the Channel Tunnel. She spoke no English when she arrived at the School, but she stayed seven years, and when she left at the age of 11 she was completely bilingual. She is now back in France, but she keeps in touch with her old school – in English!

Innovations include the extension of the number of after-school clubs, with enamelling and chess joining the longer-standing clubs like poetry, music and drama. Miss Ann (Mrs Sharp) continues to astonish with the consistent excellence of the results she achieves with those to whom she teaches the piano. A brilliant teacher, she has given much happiness and lasting joy to so many people.

The School now has an Extended Programme in which children may stay after school to play or to study. It is a facility that is helpful to parents and is appreciated by them, as are the holiday course programmes.

The staff now numbers over 60. Among them was Lady Lisle, who until her retirement in July 1995 travelled in once a week from her home in Buckinghamshire to teach scripture. She had continued to benefit the children with the wisdom of her experience and the sharpness of her mind, as she had been doing at The Hampshire School for 35 years.

Arthur Bray himself moves smoothly between the three schools, often cycling. He conducts assemblies in each building, and he uses this as teaching time, not simply as a means of giving out notices.

Arthur Bray and his staff keep abreast of the National Curriculum and nurse pupils through entrance examinations at eight, eleven, twelve and thirteen. In 1987 Penny Aitken had gained an academic scholarship to Benenden, followed by Emily Pringle's scholarship to Roedean in 1989. In 1991 Frederica West was awarded The Hampshire School's first scholarship to Wycombe Abbey when she received the Walpole Scholarship. In 1993 Crystal Whitaker became the first pupil from the Kensington Gardens School to gain a scholarship. She was awarded the Viscountess Hailsham Scholarship to The Princess Helena College.

Arthur Bray's concern is to develop the talents of all children. The closing paragraphs of the objectives he sets down in the School prospectus indicate that belief:

'Whilst constantly striving for academic excellence, staff endeavour to make learning fun and to encourage the children's confidence in their own ability. This is achieved by rewarding not only high academic attainment, but also effort, improvement and initiative; the qualities of integrity, kindness and good manners are always encouraged.

Enthusiastic participation in a wide range of activities designed to promote improved mental and physical performance is assisted and praised regardless of the level of achievement. The ability to cope with competition in all spheres of endeavour with a determined but fair approach, and to accept success or failure with equal grace, is also fostered and appreciated. Thus the School's aim is to provide an education which combines a modern approach with traditional moral values, ensuring both the toughness to cope and the tenderness to care.'

To achieve these things, a school must utilise all its assets, and Arthur Bray believes that one of the most valuable assets that a school can have is committed parental support.

In this, he echoes the words of the now legendary Miss Jane:

'The duty of any school is to produce fully rounded people who can cope in later life. Parents are equally responsible in achieving this aim. Good funding alone does not make a good school, but good teaching and care does.'

'Music Lessons!' by Uforma Ibru.

'Christmas Parties!' by Georja Calvin-Smith.

'Poetry Lessons!' by Jessica Agullo.

'Riding Weekends!' by Olivia Campbell.

Epilogue

ecent visits to The Hampshire Schools reveal places tingling with life. There is cleanliness, brightness and colour everywhere. On one wall, photographs of Miss Jane, Susan Hampshire and the tree-planting ceremony take pride of place; on another, 'Colourful Bubbles by Form One' scream at you joyfully. There are impressively attractive paintings in the styles of French Impressionist artists, inspired perhaps by recent trips to an exhibition; and there are 'les animaux de la ferme', combining the teaching of art and French.

Every classroom exudes colour and vitality, and there is the delightful atmosphere of joy in study.

There is a feeling of calm, relaxation and happiness, and there is, too, an astonishing sense of maturity. Perhaps this is not surprising when one read in the School magazine some years later that Natalie Castro had read and reviewed Vikram Seth's *A Suitable Boy* and had stated that it had made her 'wish that I could go to India and see some of the scenes from the book but it would be different because I would not be able to visit people's homes – I would just be a tourist in a hotel just looking at the outside of things'.

Marco Duyanovich's response to *Romeo and Juliet* was that Romeo 'let his emotions take over from rational behaviour', while Chloe Carapanayoti was impressed by Turgenev's *First Love*.

Richard Bray had found George Orwell's *1984* 'a brilliant book as it deals with brainwashing'. The boys, it must be remembered, were 13, Chloe was 12, and Natalie, the reader of *A Suitable Boy*, was just 11.

This was a maturity of study and of intellect that had in no way robbed these young people of their childhood. There was no distasteful precocity here.

I had met this maturity of thought several years earlier when I had been asked to judge the annual play competition at St Saviour's Hall. As a seasoned adjudicator, I did not expect too much from groups of girls, the oldest of whom was 12, but I was astonished by the programme – *1984, The Assassination of President Kennedy, The Old Woman in a Basket* – there was such variety in the seven short plays to be performed.

The smaller children began with a charming *Soldier, Soldier, Will You Marry Me?*, and we were led through various degrees of delight until we reached Form IVA and Remove's version of a scene from *1984*. The girls were dressed in grey, and they sat on chairs, imprisoned, chilling. The sensitivity and understanding of this mature and difficult book was remarkable, but even they were not the best that afternoon, although the judgement was not easy to make.

I placed first Form IIIB's *Two Little Kittens* and Miss Janice's Form IIIA for their version of Roald Dahl's *Three Little Pigs*. The characterisation was witty, the presentation was engaging and the whole performance throbbed with life. No one could have failed to enjoy it, nor to be thrilled by it.

When I stood up to make my pronouncements I was conscious not only of a sense of expectation and of excitement, but also of a warmth and a vitality. Perhaps it was that sense of *magic* that 'Miss Jane' had first encountered in those early days at St Saviour's Hall.

My judgement was later reported in the School magazine by nine-year-old Jessica Laurence. Miss Janice's form had had their panic before the competition – all good drama groups do – when Clarissa had not arrived. She was unwell, but she rallied and appeared. 'All the pigs were spectacular and the wolf and Red Riding Hood were hilarious. The chorus was good and we kept time.'

After the results were announced, 'Leila and Lupe, who were sitting next to me hugged me and squealed. I felt tremendously jubilant. Then I went home after a lovely day.'

I joined the staff for a cup of tea. They were talking about Linnet Taylor who had been offered two major scholarships, one of which was a

top scholarship to Roedean. Miss Jane was explaining what Linnet had
done and why she had made such a good and deep impression. The
discussion was exhilarating.

There was pride in achievement, but there was deep concern for others. The atmosphere was shot with that spark of electricity of which I had
been conscious all morning. I felt honoured to be part of it, however
briefly.

The ability to inspire pupils is of the utmost importance in achieving
a successful school and, as Sir Anthony Dowell says in his Foreword, to
teach and instil a sense of self-discipline. This history also illustrates
the importance of ideals, and why they should not be lost within ever-
changing educational theories. It also records the landmarks of the
School's progress over 67 years – establishment of the studio in
Knightsbridge in 1932; the move to St Saviour's Hall in 1946; the purchase of 63 Ennismore Gardens in 1969; foundation of L'Ecole
Hampshire in France in 1977–78; full accreditation of the School in
1985; the expansion of the pupil roll and premises under the ownership
of Nord Anglia Education PLC from 1987 to the present day. And the
work of the 50th Anniversary Educational Trust should not be forgotten.
But perhaps the greatest achievement of all has been that pupils and parents remember that they were treated fairly, and their abilities were
encouraged and nurtured.

I think that this history reveals that exemplary ideals together with a
fresh vision of education were translated into positive success. I hope
that readers will admire, as I do, this history of development and achievement – which began in the drawing-room of a house in Surrey all those
years ago.

The Hampshire School 50th Anniversary Educational Trust

Registered Charity Number 280556

65 Pelham Court, 145 Fulham Road, London SW3 6SH

Telephone & Fax: 0171-584 0744

We, the Trustees, do hope you have enjoyed reading how the original vision of The Hampshire Schools was achieved. Now we are looking forward to the millennium and visions for the future. We would like to ask for your suggestions and active help.

The first objective of our Deed of Trust is stated as the advancement of education in connection with The Hampshire Schools – and, since mid-1980, more than £35,000 has been awarded to many pupils and former pupils in the shape of scholarships, prizes and grants. We shall, of course, continue to make these awards but we are also looking to launch new and exciting visions for the future. We must always keep in mind what we call the 'three-E' concept – education, environment and entertainment – and direct our efforts to offer maximum support to the children of tomorrow. A number of schemes are being studied – examples being a country nature reserve, small theatre and rehearsal studio in London, and radio programmes for and by children, to name but three. We would welcome ideas and suggestions from children and parents.

We can only achieve new 'visions' for the future with your generous help. You will be aware that there are several methods of giving support which allow individuals and companies to make tax-effective donations to charity. Donors and the Trust derive maximum benefit from deeds of covenant, participation in 'Gift Aid' and 'Give As You Earn' schemes, bequests through wills and other means.

Details of such methods of giving towards the achievement of new 'visions' can be obtained from our Hon. Administrator at the above address.

The great Winston Churchill once said 'We make a living by what we get, but we make a life by what we give.'

His wise words are even more relevant today.

Illustrations by current pupils of The Hampshire Schools.

Roll of Former Pupils
1928—1987, London and Surrey

Unfortunately, during the moves from the Basil Street Studio and St Saviour's Hall, a number of registers and other key records were lost or destroyed. Therefore, this roll cannot be as comprehensive as we would wish and we can only apologise for any inaccuracies or omissions.

ABDUL AZIZ, Maha
ABDUL AZIZ, Shadha
ABEL, Gillian
ABEL, Quinten
ABLITT, Carolyn
ABRAMOWICZ, Agnes
ABUSAMRA, Reem
ABUSAMRA, Roula
ADAMS, Antonia
ADAMS, Louisa
ADAMS, Suzy
ADAMS, Victoria
ADEANE, Dorelia
ADDIS, Catherine
ADDIS, Charles
ADDIS, Claire
ADDIS, Elizabeth
AGNEW, Charles
AGNEW, Jeremy
AGULLO, Jessica
AGULLO, Nuria
AHMAD, Ashee
AILION, Anita

AITCHISON, Alexandra
AITCHISON, Ann
AITCHISON, Emily
AITCHISON, Eveline
AITCHISON, Victoria
AITKEN, Alexandra
AITKEN, Fiona
AITKEN, Georgiana
AITKEN, Lucinda
AITKEN, Penelope
AITKEN, Sarah
AITKEN, Alexandra
AITKEN, Victoria
AITKEN, William
AL ASKARI, Omar
AL ASKARI, Taymour
AL ASKARI, Maya
AL ATIA, Rana
AL ATIA, Zainab
ALDERSLEY WILLIAMS,
   Hugh
ALGHARBALLY, Abeer
ALGHARBALLY, Yousef

ALI KHAN, Maryam
ALI KHAN, Zainab
AL KHALIFA, Alia
AL KHALIFA, Latifu
AL KHASTAI, Saud
AL KHASTAI, Walid
AL KOTUBI, Dana
ALLEN, Christopher
ALLEN, Dana
ALLEN, Elizabeth
ALLEN, Kristen
ALLEN, Rosemary
ALLEN, Sarah
AL MANSOURI, Dena
AL MANSOURI, Khaled
AL MULLA, Avan
AL MULLA, Shlair
AL MUMIN, Manar
AL MUMIN, Maysaa
AL MUMIN, Munthir
AL MURBARAK, Ali
AL RAYES, Talal
AL SABAH, Ahmed

AL SABAH, Merieam
AL SABAH, Sabah
AL SABAH, Sundus
AL SHAWI, Manat
AL TOBAISHI, Narwal
ALVARADO, Olivia
ALWAN, Alia
ALWAN, Natalie
ALYAMANI, Susan
AMERI, Sanaz
AMON, Lindsay
AMUKA PEMU, Nicola
ANDERSON, Joan
ANDERSON, Karen
ANDERSON, Kathy
ANNAND, Charlotte
ANTHILL, Audrey
ANTHILL, Mavis
AOKI, Echo
AOKI, Meiko
APPELBEE, Jane
APTEKMAN, Olivia
ARRAS, Leticia
ARKELL, Amanda
ARKELL, Simon
ARLETT, Sandra
ARMACOST, Elizabeth
ARMACOST, Susan
ARMITAGE, Caroline
ARMITAGE, Rose
ARMITAGE, William
ARMSTRONG-
    McDONNELL, Susan
ARNOLD-BAKER,
    Henry
ASCHAN, Patrick
ASHTON, Tessa
ASHTON, Vivien
ASHTON-BOSTOCK,
    Sophie
ATTARA, Michael
AVRAAMIDES, Paris
AWAK, Ryan
AWAK, Zainab
AYACHE, Munthir
AYACHE, Nadine
AYNETCHI, Ladan

AZAGURY, Gabrielle
AZAGURY, Michelle
AZEM, Karim
AZEM, Samer

BABCOCK, Glenys
BADEN, John
BAILLIE, Kitty
BAILLIE, Sarah
BAIRD, Page
BAKER, Euphemia
BAKER, Leo Marshall
BAKER, Emma
BALDO, Gabriel
BALL, Benjamin
BANKS, Miranda
BANKS, Sinclair
BARCLAY, Amanda
BARCLAY, Carey
BARKER, Georgina
BARKER, Nicholas
BARKER-MILL, Isolde
BARNES, Sarah
BARRATT, Kimberley
BARTLETT, Henrietta
BARTLETT, Leonora
BARWICK, Victoria
BASSANTE, Reem
BASTIN, Alexander
BATCHELOR, Janet
BATCHELOR, Mark
BATHURST, Linda
BATTELLO, Claudia
BATTING, Richard
BATTY, Charles
BAYLEY, Richard
BAYLISS, Caroline
BAXTER-COOPER,
    Justine
BAZZOCCHI, Chiara
BEBBEHANI, Boudour
BEBBEHANI, Mona
BECKETT, Sarah
BECKWITH, Patricia
BEDEL, Geraldine
BEDEL, Laetitia
BEGG, Alexandra

BEGG, Victoria
BEHRMANN, Marisa
BEHZADI, Susan
BELL, Henrietta
BELLARA, Koushal
BELLINGHAM, Hannah
BEMBRIDGE, Jennifer
BENNETT, Victoria
BENNETT, Zaffran
BENSON, Dorian
BERADO, Karin
BERGER, Elizabeth
BERGGREN, Jacqueline
BERGNE, Louise
BERGUNO, Alexandra
BERNSTROM,
    Stephanie
BERTISH, Susannah
BERTRAM, Lavinia
BESKIN, Barbara
BESSON, Aquiles
BESSON, Carola
BEVAN, Anna
BEVAN, Henrietta
BEYFUS, Jane
BHOJWANI, Nafeez
BIDDLE, Catherine
BIDDLE, Lydia
BILIMATSIS, Maria
BILLSON, Annabel
BILLSON, Alexis
BINSTOCK, Jonathan
BINSTOCK, Nathalie
BINSTOCK, Richard
BLACKBURN, Jonathan
BLACKBURN, Lucy
BLAKER, Adam
BLAKER, Candida
BLAKER, Helena
BLAKER, Bettina
BLAKER, Marie-Louise
BLAMEY, Emma
BLECHNER, Irene
BLOMFIELD, Anna
BLOMPIED, Viviana
BLOOMER, Katie
BLYSTONE, Daniel

BLYSTONE, Julia
BOASE, Rachel
BOISSET, Anita
BONE, Lesley
BONGARD, Anna
BONGARD, Gaynor
BONGARD, Sara
BONVIN, Odette
BOOTH, Rebecca
BORTHWICK, John
BOSS, Dominic
BOTSFORD, Clarissa
BOTSFORD, Giannandrea
BOTT, David
BOTTS, Amanda
BOTTS, Sarah
BOUTON, Ligia
BOUTON, Shannon
BOWDEN, Annette
BOX, Clarissa
BOX-GRAINGER, Eve
BOX-GRAINGER, Jill
BOX-GRAINGER, Paul
BOZOKY, Sarah
BOZOKY, Zoltan
BRADDOCK, Timothy
BRAITHWAITE, John
BRAMPTON, Annabel
BRAMPTON, Claudine
BRANCH, Anna
BRANCH, Lisa
BRATT, Duncan
BRATT, Sarah
BRAY, Katherine
BRAY, Richard
BRENNAN, Sophie
BRETT-SMITH, Jerome
BRETT-SMITH, Odette
BRIANT, Julien
BRIGGS, Marnie
BRITTAIN-CATLIN,
    Larissa
BROACKES, Simon
BROACKES, Victoria
BROGGER, Christine
BROGGER, Gregory
BROGGER, Karen

BROMOVSKY, Francis
BROOKE POWELL,
    Alexandra
BROOKER, Nella
BROUGHTON, Gemma
BROUGHTON, Michael
BROWN, Eugenie
BRUCE, Catriona
BRYERS, Adrian
BUBEAR, Annabel
BUCCALOSSI, Annalisa
BUCCALOSSI, Paola
BUCHANAN, Marisa
BUCKLAND, Tiffany
BUHLER, Michael
BUJARRABAL, Ana
BUJARRABAL, Laura
BUJARRABAL, Rocio
BUNDAY, Gylda
BUNYAN, John
BUNYAN, Peter
BURCHELL, Alison
BURGESS, James
BURGIN, Janice
BURGIN, Suzanne
BURGIN, Yolande
BURKE, Janina
BURKE, Richard
BURROWS, Donalee
BURT, Alexandra
BURT, James
BURTON, Michael
BURTON, Sophie
BUSI, Elizabeth
BUSK, Camilla
BUTCHER, Katriona
BUTCHER, Natalie
BYERS, Elizabeth

CABRITA, Patricia
CALO, Paola
CAMPBELL, Iris
CAMPBELL, Malcolm
CAMPBELL, Olivia
CAMPOS, Thelma
CANTWELL, Tina
CAPARROS, Elizabeth

CAPARROS, Marie-Laure
CAPON, Tara
CARDWELL, Amynta
CARNEY, Abigail
CARR, Lorna
CARRELL, Dorian
CARRINGTON, Jennifer
CARROLL, Brian
CARROLL, Celia
CARROLL, Daphne
CARRUTHERS, Quinton
CARTWRIGHT, Isobel
CARVALHO, Christine
CARVALHO, Richard
CARVER, Alice
CARVER, Richard
CASSANDRO, Adriana
CASTILLO, Gabriella
CASTILLO, Tito
CASTRO NEVES, Carlos
CASTRO NEVES, Luiz
CATTO, Ariane
CAULFIELD, Anne Marie
CESSFORD, Diana
CEVAHIR, Elif
CEVAHIR, Gulen
CHALLIS, Laura
CHAMBERS, Lucinda
CHAMBERS, Rourden
CHAN, Arnold
CHAN, Fiona
CHAN, Reynold
CHANDLER, Joan
CHAPMAN, Kia
CHAPPLE, Amy
CHAPPLE, Jessica
CHARLES, Katriona
CHARLES, Lucy
CHAVES, Lesley
CHAVES, Lorna
CHEATLE, Sandra Mary
CHEBARO, Sarna
CHEN, Diane
CHERECK, Robert
CHESTER, Melanie
CHESTON, Dena
CHESTON, Rebecca

CHILD-VILLIERS, Alexander
CHILD-VILLIERS, Roderick
CHOW, Brian
CHOW, Cindy
CHURCH, Annabel
CHURCH, Carolyn
CHURCH, Henrietta
CLAPP, Ariel
CLARK, Kathryn
CLARK, Kim
CLARK, Kristen
CLEVENGER, Anne
CLINKARD, Victoria
CLIVE, Ludmilla
CLOYD, David
COBB, Shelley
COBB, Susan
COHEN, Eran
COHEN, Nirit
COHEN, Philippa
COLERIDGE, Christine
COLES, Richard
COLES, Alison
COLES, Caroline
COLES, Isabel
COLINVAUX, Roger
COLLINS, Jane
COLLINGS-BECKMAN, Marisa
COLLIS, David
COLVIN, Siri
COMYN, Kate
CONLON, Christine
CONNELL, Stephanie
CONTE, Aurelia
CONYERS, James
CONYNGHAM, Henrietta
CONYNGHAM, Wolfe
CONZE, Nicola
COOK, Alexander
COOK, Francesca
COOMBE, Lachlan
COOMBS, Andrew
COOPER, Elizabeth
COOPER, Marilyn

COOPER, Sheila
COOPER, Wendy
COOTE, Nicola
CORDOVA, Roberta
COULSON, Amanda
COULTER, Claire
COULTER, Primrose
COURTNEY KRUTA, Lauren
COWIN, Lois
COWIN, Maurice
CRAIG, Jacaranda
CRAIG-RAYMOND, Tay
CRAIGIE, Gail
CRAMPTON SMITH, Fiona
CRAMPTON SMITH, Gillian
CRANDALL, John
CREGAN, Amanda
CREGAN, Shaun
CROCKER, Elizabeth
CROFTON, Georgiana
CROMARTIE, Alan
CROMARTIE, Selina
CROMARTIE, Serena
CUDDY, Shawn
CULBERT, Jennifer
CULLEN, Serena
CUNLIFFE, Robert
CURLING, Antonia
CURLING, Charlotte
CURRIE, Alisdair
CURRIE, James
CURRIE, Piers
CUTMORE, Nicholas
CSAKY, Lela
CZETWERTYNSKI, Alexander

DA COSTA, Renato
DAHL, Candida
DAHL, Jessica
DA LAMAL, Maresh
DALBY, Amanda
DANBY, Nicola
DANIELS, Michelle

D'ANTONIO, Chiara
DARBYSHIRE, Alexandra
DARBYSHIRE, Gabrielle
DARWISH, Razan
DARWISH, Shaima
DA SILVA CLAMP, Andrew
DA SILVA CLAMP, James
DA SILVA CLAMP, Jonathan
DATTA, Roopa
DAVENPORT, Sara
DAVIDSON, Bettina
DAVIS, Emma
DAVIS, Jaimee
DAVIS, Katy
de BARANDICA, Beatriz
de CADENET, Amanda
de CHAMBERET, Georgia
DEADMAN, Jake
DEAKIN, Johnny
DECKER, Laura
DEFRIES, Fleur
DEGENHARDT, Sophia
de GUTTADAUKE, Andrea
de HAAN, Alexandra
de HORSEY, Ann
de HORSEY, Jane
de JERSEY LOWNEY, Claire
DELAMAIN, Georgina
DEL GUIDICE, Scott
DELISLE, Annabel
de LISO, Raffaella
DELL, Robin
de LOTBINIERE, Christine
de LOTBINIERE, Pauline
de LUPIS, Christine
de LUPIS, Lawrence
de LUPIS, Nicholas
de LUPIS, Peter
DEMAN, Humphrey
DEMARKIS, Deidre
DEMARKIS, John
DENNISON, Lisa
de OYZABAL, Marta

de OYZABAL, Matilda
de PICCOLI, Nadia
DESCHAMPNEUFS,
    Frances
de SMET, Felice
DEVAS, Emma
DEVAS, Esmond
DEVAS, Prosper
DEVILLAVILLA, Alexander
DEVILLAVILLA, Sasha
de WARDENER, Simon
DEYT AYSAGE, Dorothy
DIAB, Aly
DIAL, Elizabeth
DIBA, Cathy
DIBBEN, Gye
DIERKS, Michael
DIPPLE, Amelia
DIPPLE, Richard
DOBSON, Toby
DODSON, Danielle
DOMINGUEZ, Isabel
DONALDSON, Andrew
DONALDSON, Frances
DONALDSON, Richard
DONNER, Cassandra
DOOLEY, Helen
DOUGLAS, Amanda
DOUGLAS, Angus
DOUGLAS, Rowan
DOUGLAS, Timothy
DOUGLAS MANN, Lucy
DOUTHETT, Gabrielle
DOWELL, Anthony
DOWELL, Carole
DOWN, Melinda
DOWNIE, John
DOXAT, Sandra
D'OYLY, Sherry
DU CANN, Charlotte
DU CANN, Christian
DU CANN, Matthew
DU CANN, Ruth
DUCHATEAU, Martin
DUDLEY SMITH, Antonia
DUDLEY SMITH,
    Charlotte

DUNBAR-MILLER,
    Alexandra
DUNPHY, Rachel
du PONT de BIE, Natacha
du PONT de BIE, Rebecca
DURLACHER, Samantha
du ROURET, Axelle
de ROURET, Caroline
DUVALL, Terence
DUVOLLET-LYNCH,
    Angela
DWYER, Gabrielle

EADIE, Toby
EARLE, Cordelia
EARLE, Kate
EARLE, Lucy
EDMONDSON, Peta
EDU, Remi
EDWARDS, Anna
EDWARDS, Gemma
EDWARDS, George
EGAN, Laurie Ann
EGBERTS, Hendriques
EL HADJ, Alan
EL HADJ, Alec
EL HADJ, David
EL HADJ, Elissa
EL HADJ, Michael
ELLIOTT, Anthony
ELLIOTT, Kathryn
ELLIOTT, Meg
ELLIOTT, Rosemary
EL RAYES, Sarah
ELRICK, Susan
ELSAWY, Sara
ELWES, Annabel
EMPSON, Paul
ENDERS, Alexandra
ENGEL, Elizabeth
ENGLISH, Charlotte
ENSTONE, David
ERWIN, James
ESCOTT, Harry
ESCOTT, Jonathan
ESCOTT, Sarah
E SILVA, Beatriz

ESTES, Brandei
ESTLER, Toby
EVANS, Clare
EVANS, Jennifer
EVANS, Nancy
EYLER, Jeanne

FABER, Susan
FACEY, Blake
FAGERNAS, Sonia
FAIRER SMITH, Robert
FALCE, Anthony
FALCE, Caroline
FALLON, Joanna
FARGE, James
FARNON, Catherine
FARNON, Celia
FARNON, Peter
FAROOKI, Kiron
FAROOKI, Preeti
FAROOKI, Roopa
FARRELL, Sara
FATTORINI, Katherine
FATTORINI, Matthew
FAUST, Alex
FEHR, Olinda
FEI, Mark
FEDERMAN, Belle
FERGUSON, Elizabeth
FERGUSON, Mead
FIECHTER, Bettina
FILLIMORE, Joel
FINCH, Anita
FIRTH, Harriet
FIRTH, Katie
FISCHEL, Marian
FISHER, Francesca
FITCH, Angela
FLETCHER, Susie
FOGARTY, John
FOOKS, Charlotte
FORD, Alicia
FOROUGHI, Mandana
FOROUGHI, Roxanne
FOROUGHI, Shahran
FORREST, Emma
FOULSHAM, Ann

FOWLER, Alison
FRAIMAN, Nerida
FRANK, Sophie
FRANKLIN, Jasmine
FRANKLIN, Jennifer
FRANKLIN, Katherine
FRANSIOLI, Christina
FRASER, Jacqueline
FRASER, Penny
FRASISTI, Marianna
FRASISTI, Vanessa
FREER, Elizabeth
FREER, Isabel
FRENCH, Nicholas
FRENCH, Winston
FRERICHS, Elizabeth
FREWIN, Elke
FRITH, Alexander
FRITTS, Jean
FRITTS, Katherine
FULLER, Catherine
FURNEAUX, Victoria
FURNELL, Susan
FURTADO, Navin
FURTADO, Udhay

GABILONDO, Maria
GADD, Caroline
GALBERG, Susan
GALE, Marie
GALITZINE, Nicolai
GALLAGHER, Michelle
GALLAGHER, Siobhan
GALLIGAN, Alexandra
GALVIN, Susan
GALVIN, Vincent
GARMAN, Elizabeth
GARRICK, Annette
GARRICK, Louella
GARROW, Annabel
GARROW, Julie
GEDDES, Alison
GEDDES, Duncan
GEDDES, Lindsey
GEE, Caroline
GEE, Philippa
GEIKIE, Carol

GENCK, Frederic
GENCK, Lauren
GENTLE, Aletheia
GENTLE, Henry
GEORGE, Camilla
GEORGE, Simon
GERSBACH, Marcus
GHAFFARI, Amir
GHAFFARI, Bahar
GHAFFARI, Saghi
GHAFFARI, Shahzrad
GHANAM, Amira
GHARABALLY, Abeer
GIBBS, Camilla
GIELGUD, Maina
GILDERSLEEVE, Oliver
GILKES, Nicola
GILKES, Simon
GILLIATT, Anne Louise
GILLIATT, Sophie
GILMORE, Natasha
GITTINS, Cheryl
GLAZEBROOK, Lucy
GLEAVE, Karen
GOLD, Alyson
GOLD, Emma
GOLDSTEIN, Jennifer
GONZALEZ, Fabio
GONZALEZ, John
GONZALEZ, Marianna
GOODMAN, Anna
GOODMAN, Kia
GOODMAN, Rebecca
GOODRIDGE, Kate
GOODWIN, Jason
GOODWIN, Penny
GOODWIN, Sabine
GORDON, Ace
GORDON, Claudine
GORDON, Olivia
GORDON, Trilby
GORMAN, Annabel
GORMAN, Caroline
GORMAN, Jennifer
GORZALY, Marianna
GOURGEY, Clare
GOURGEY, David

GOURGEY, Gabrielle
GRAEME, Gillian
GRAHAM, Frances
GRAHAM GREENISH,
    Davinia
GRAHAM GREENISH,
    Desireé
GRAHAM HALL,
    Margarethy
GRANIER-DEFERRE,
    Christopher
GRANT, Hannah
GRANT PETERKIN,
    Alexandra
GRANT PETERKIN,
    James
GRAVER, Julia
GREATREX, Deborah
GREATREX, Louisa
GREEN, Christine
GREENE, Aubrey
GREENE, Joanna
GREENE, John
GREENE, Teresa
GREENHILL, Nigel
GREENWOOD, Patricia
GREEVEN, Amely
GREEVEN, Caroline
GRENIER, Paola
GRIFFIN, Christian
GRIFFIN, Tessa
GRIFFITHS, Carolyn
GRIFFITHS, Christian
GRIFFITHS, Diana
GRIFFITHS, Emma
GRIFFITHS, Lucy
GRIFFITHS, Max
GRIFFITHS, Simon
GRISWOLD, Kathy
GRISWOLD, Sarah
GROGAN, Kathryn
GROGAN, Sarah
GROOM, Sophie
GROSZEK, Alexandra
GUERLAIN, Claire
GUERLAIN, Marie
GUERRA, Mania

GULABANI, Marika
GURIAN, Peter
GUTHRIE, Alexander
GUTHRIE, Linnet
GUZELIAN, Arminé
GUZELIAN, Kariné
GWILLIAM, Faith
GWILLIAM, Hilary
GWYNN, Francesca

HACK, Jonathan
HACK, Samantha
HACK, Toby
HADID, Tala
HAILSTONE, Jessica
HAILSTONE, Susanna
HALBY, Kim
HALBY, Margaret
HALBY, Robin
HALL, Katrina
HALL, Margaret
HALLWACHS, Marianna
HALLWACHS, Winifred
HALPIN, Emma
HALPIN, Deborah
HALPIN, Nicholas
HASLEY, Joscelin
HAMBLEN, Nicholas
HAMILTON, David
HAMILTON, Susannah
HAMLYN, Jane
HAMLYN, William
HAMMAN, Nermin
HAMPSHIRE, Daniel
HAMPSHIRE, Susan
HANDHAL, Rasha
HARA, Safiyeh
HARB, Jawad
HARB, Karma
HARKNESS, Alison
HARKNESS, Josephine
HARLAND, Thomas
HARRINGTON, William
HARRIS, Georgina
HARRYHAUSEN, Vanessa
HARTNELL, Peter
HARWOOD, Sophie

HASHIO, Kazuko
HASSETT, Doon
HATCHWELL, Christine
HAUSER, Clara
HAWKE, Belinda
HAWKES, Eleanor
HAWKES, Katherine
HEADLAM, Caroline
HEADLAM, Hugo
HEALEY, Sophie
HEARD, Edith
HEATHMAN, Rebecca
HEGG, Kaja
HEGG, Thea
HEGG, Ulla
HEINRICH, Marion
HELAS, Karim
HELLIESEN, Nina
HELM, Petrina
HEMMINGS, Nolan
HENDERSON, Catriona
HENDERSON, Edwina
HENDERSON, Elizabeth
HENDERSON, Penelope
HENDERSON, Gavin
HENSLEY, Caroline
HENSLEY, Gerald
HENRY, Katherine
HENTY, Rose
HERMAN, Virena
HERSHBERGER, Richard
HERVEY, Mavis
HESKETH, Arabella
HETREED, Juliet
HEWENS, Lucy
HEWENS, Nicholas
HINCHCLIFFE, Graham
HICKEY, Patrick
HICKS, Christopher
HIGGS, Julia
HIDALGO, Thomas
HILDRETH, Duke
HILDRETH, Jane
HILL, Margaret
HILL, Rupert
HILLMAN EADIE, Belinda
HINTON, Jane Ann

HIRSCH, Rufus
HIXON, Jennifer
HOARE, Benjamin
HOARE, Richard
HOCKEY, Rose
HODGKINSON, Jane
HOGAN, Kate
HOGARTH, James
HOLE, Max
HOLLEY TAYLOR, Tracey
HOLMAN, Adams
HOLMAN, Hilary
HOLT, Charlotte
HOLT, Georgina
HOLT, Michael
HOOKER, Benjamin
HOOKER, Samantha
HOPEWELL-ASH,
    Catherine
HORNBY, Melinda
HORNBY, Patricia
HORSFALL, Gail
HORTA, Liz
HOTCHKIN, Sarah
HOURANI, Amer
HOURANI, Nael
HOURANI, Suha
HOVELL, Devika
HOWARD, Amanda
HOWARD, Camilla
HOWCROFT, Debby
HOWELL, Lisa
HOWELL, Thekla
HOWELL, William
HOYER-MILLAR, Eliza
HUDSON, Helena
HUDSON, Karina
HUDSPETH, Elizabeth
HüLSEBUS, Kristina
HULT, Heine
HULTGREN, Meredith
HUMPHRIS, Nicolas
HUNT, Nicola Novello
HUNTER, Gwen
HUNTER, Julie
HUNTER, Katherine
HYKAL, George

HYKAL, Jimmy
HYMAN, Daphne

IBANEZ-MARTIN, Ana
IBANEZ-MARTIN, Rocio
IBANEZ-MARTIN, Rosita
IBRU, Uforma
INBAR, Daniella
IND, Charles
IND, Thomas
INGRAM, Elizabeth
INGRAM, Francesca
INGRAM, Sherilyn
ISRAEL, Brett
ISRAEL, Darien
IVALDI, Lisa
IVESHA, Natalie
IWANAGA, Yoichi
IZADI, Nilufar

JABER, Kamel
JACK, Nicholas
JACKSON, Caroline
JACKSON, Jane
JACKSON, Louisa
JACKSON, Peter
JAGGER, Anthony
JAMES, Joanna
JAMES, Philippa
JAMES, Lawrence
JAMESON, Ian
JAMESON, Jane
JARDINE, Nicola
JAUREQUI, Giselle
JEFFERIES, Charles
JEFFERY, Heather
JEFFERY, Richard
JENKINS, Chloe
JENKINS, Joanne
JENKS, Emma
JENSEN, Kristen
JEPSON, Gillian
JEPSON-TURNER, Belita
JOB, Charlotte
JOB, Rivers
JOHNSON, Carol Ann
JOHNSON, Cynthia

JOHNSON, Dikon
JOHNSON, Hilarie
JOHNSON, Lief
JOHNSON, Melinda
JONES, Brian
JONES, Jordan
JORDAN, Charles
JORDAN, Kathy
JORDAN, Stephen
JORDAO, Joanna
JOSEPHSON, Jennie
JREDINI, Carl
JREDINI, Marc
JUDAH, Samuel

KABIR, Heba
KALLA, Joudi
KALLA, Lara
KALLA, Maya
KALLA, Tanya
KAMURAS, Emanuel
KASSARDJIAN, Tamara
KATZ, Jody
KAUFFMAN, Scott
KAWAKATSU, Chikayo
KAWAKATSU, Hideki
KAYYALI, Kinda
KAYYALI, Randa
KAZAN, Michael
KEEN, Colette
KEIL, Justin
KEIL, Samantha
KEIL, Susannah
KEIR CROSS, Jennifer
KELLEHER, Lauren
KELSON, Anthony
KEMENY, Susan
KEMP, Andrew
KEMP, Yolande
KENNEDY, Emma
KENRICK, Emma
KHAN, Shamin
KHAN KASSAM, Aly
KHAN KASSAM, Salima
KHATER, Sarah
KHATOUM, Bassel
KHAYAMI, Alidad

KHAYATT, Dima
KHAZAM, Hilde-Ann
KHOURY, Jean
KHOURY, Rami
KIDD, Sally
KING, Judy
KINN, Rachel
KINNA, Sophie
KIRCHNER, Felicity
KIRKWOOD, Lauren
KITSON, Emma
KLEANTHOUS, Andrea
KLEANTHOUS, Anna
KLINGER, Anthony
KNAPP, David
KNIGHT, Victoria
KOCHAR, Ashwani
KOCH DE
    GOOREYEND, Stella
KONIG, Serena
KOTECHA, Hema
KOTLER, Liane
KROL, Monika
KUFFERMAN, Lindsey
KUHNE, Inger
KULICK, Thea
KUNCAR, Katherina
KUNCAR, Suzanne
KUNSTADTER, Elizabeth
KUTAY, Orhan
KUTAY, Perihan

LADD, Kellian
LADD, Tracy
LA DELL, Tom
LAING, Alistair
LAING, Niall
LAING, Pamela
LAK, Leila
LAK, Naz
LALVANI, Divyia
LAMBERT, Rose
LAMBRAKIS, Alexandra
LAMBRAKIS, Frederique
LAMKI, Maha
LAMKI, Roya
LAMKI, Saud

LAMPSON, Edith
LANCASTER, Bettina
LANCASTER, Deborah
LANGDON, Nicola
LAPATI, Gaudalupe
LAPATI, Mariana
LARCHER, Elizabeth
LARDNER BURKE,
    Amanda
LARDNER BURKE, Clare
LARSON, Gretchen
LASSELLE, Catherine
LAUPRETRE, Guillaume
LAURENCE, Charles
LAURENCE, Kate
LAURENCE, Jessica
LAURENCE, Rebecca
LAWDER, Joan
LAWS, Margaret Grace
LAWSON, Stuart
LAZELL, Natasha
LEA, Georgina
LEACH, Philippa
LEAPMAN, Emma
LEAPMAN, Joanna
LE BLANC, Eric
LE BLANC, Michelle
LEE, Ann Gary
LEE, Adrian
LEE, Melinda
LEE, Meriel
LEE, Christina
LEE, Jessy
LEE, Pearl
LEIGH, Sarah Jane
LE MIEUX, Babette
LE MIEUX, Jolie
LENZI, Jacopi
LEON, Susan
LERNER, Joel
LESS, Michelle
LESSALL, Matthew
LESTER, Anne
LESTER, Mylan
L'ESTRANGE, Minette
LEVELLE, James
LEVINE, Kari

LEVINE, Ronnie
LEVY, Jasmin
LEWIS, Win
LEY GREAVES, Beth
LEY GREAVES, Susan
LIDDLE, Juliet
LIEBERSON, Lucy
LING, Selina
LING, Victoria
LITLAND, Jon
LIUZZI, Clementina
LIUZZI, Rafaella
LIVINGSTON, Hamel
LIVINGSTONE, Hannah
LLEWELLYN-DAVIS,
    Henrietta
LOCK, Isabella
LODER, Christina
LODER, Timothy
LOGIE, Mark
LOGIE, Marina
LOOST, Nicola
LORD, Amanda
LORD, Caroline
LORD, Emma
LORD, Rosemary
LORD, Simon
LORENCO, Jorge
LORENZATOS, Pierette
LOVELL, Claire
LOVELL, Jonathan
LOWDER, Rupert
LOWENTHAL, Anna
LOWENTHAL, Sarah
LOWSLEY WILLIAMS, Toby
LUBIN, Luisa
LUCAS-BOX, Fabergé
LUCE, Paola
LUKE, Alexandra
LUKE, Nicholas
LUSH, Amanda
LUSH, Deborah
LUSH, Jonathan
LYNCH, Sean
LYON, Charlotte
LYONS, Deborah

MAASARANI, Eman
MacARTHUR, Anna
MacARTHUR, Jane
MacARTHUR, Niall
MACARTNEY, Annabella
MACHADO, Helen
MACHADO, Rita
MACINTOSH, Catriona
MACINTOSH, Fiona
MACOMBER, Maclise
MACONOCHIE, James
MACONOCHIE, Sophie
MACONOCHIE, Tracy
MACKAY-LEWIS, Michael
MACKAY-LEWIS, Mourne
McCOMBE, Kirsty
McCORQUODALE, Iona
McCORQUODALE, Tara
McCOLL, Amanda
McCOLL, Sarah
McCORMICK GOOD-
    HEART, Henrietta
McCRAE, Brian
McCRAE, Heather
McCRAE, Paul
McDONALD, Marnie
McDONNELL, Conrad
McDONNELL, Constance
McDONNELL, William
McGEE, David
McGEE, Suzanne
McGILDOWNEY, Marina
McGOWAN, Heather
McGOWAN, Jacqueline
McGUIRK, Brendan
McHATTON, Anna
McIVER, Gillian
McKAY, Catriona
McKAY, Charlotte
McKAY, Samuel
McLAREN, Anne
McLEAN, Mark
McMILLAN, Thomas
McMORREN, Nema
McORAN CAMPBELL,
    Adrian
McORAN CAMPBELL,
    Fiona

McORAN CAMPBELL, James
McWHIRTER, Catherine
MACOWAN, Rachel
MAGER, Emma
MAHZARI, Yasmin
MAILA, Yasmine
MAILLARD, Julie
MAITLAND, Madeleine
MAKHZANI, Atin
MALEKI, Bahareh
MALHOTRA, Sujata
MALIK-NOOR, Sasha
MALLINSON-MATHEW, Charlotte
MALTBY, Alan
MALTBY, Niall
MALTBY, Timothy
MANDEL, Audrey
MANDEL, Marcia
MANGIN, Louis
MANGIN, Virginie
MANKIEWIEZ, Alexandra
MANLEY, Dominic
MANLEY, Edward
MANN, Aran
MANN, Jessie
MANNERS, Moira
MANNERS, Phoebe
MANNING, Alistair
MANNING, Angeline
MANNING, Melissa
MANSOUR, Gina
MAPPIN, John
MAPPIN, Nicholas
MARAL, Camilla
MARCET, Camilla
MARCHANT, Pat
MARET, Susan
MARK, Lisa
MARKS, Amanda
MARKS, Sarah
MARLOWE, Rebecca
MARIGGI, Elena
MARRIOTT, Benjamin
MARRIS, Caroline
MARSHALL, Margaret

MARTIN, Charlotte
MARTIN, Giles
MARTINEZ-CASTRO, Alex
MASON, Sandra
MASON, William
MASSER, Penelope
MASSER, Sally
MASSER, Simon
MASSIMI, Michael
MASTERS, Lara
MASTROJANI, Carlotta
MASTROJANI, Francesca
MASUREL, Anne-Sophie
MATAR, Daniella
MATAR, Joella
MATAR, Lara
MATHEWS, Heather
MAVROLEON, Irene
MAYERSBERG, Natasha
MAYS, Sarah
MAXWELL, Charles
MEAKIN, Peter
MEDAK, Karen
MEDANI, Barmak
MELICH, Tanya
MELLEGARD, Vivecca
MELLOAN, Maryanne
MELVILLE, Fleur
MELWANI, Bimal
MELWANI, Meetu
MELZAK, Sophie
MENCKOFF, Christina
MENZIES, Anoushka
MESHIEA, Abdul Aziz
MESSERLIAN, Fiona
METCALFE, Charles
METTA, Jimmy
METTA, Roger
MEYNELL, Katherine
MIERS, Claire
MILLER, Andrew
MILLER, Gretchen
MILLER, Katherine
MILLER, Leila
MILLER, Lindsay
MILLER, Lucy

MILLER, Michelle
MILLER, Sally
MILLS, Harriet
MILLS, Miranda
MILLS, Samantha
MILNE, Catherine
MILNE, Nicholas
MILNE, Sarah
MILNE, Simon
MILTON, Charles
MILTON, Joanna
MILTON, Philippa
MIMS, Kimberley
MIRFAKHARI, Susan
MITCHELL, Holly
MITCHELL, Rebecca
MODJAHEDI, Susan
MOELLER, Beatrice
MOITA, Francisco
MOITA, Patricia
MOLDAVI, Barbak
MOLDAVI, Miriam
MONADJEMI, Parisa
MONRO, Douglas
MONRO, Heather
MONTALETTE, Bettina
MONTANARI, Christine
MONTANARI, Ivan
MONTANARO, Fleur
MONTASHAMI, Nanaz
MOORE, Charlotte
MOORE, Natasha
MORGAN, Andrew
MORGAN, Camilla
MORGAN, David
MORGAN, Louise
MORGAN, Lucy
MORGAN, Stephanie
MORLEY-PEGG, Ingrid
MORTON, Hugh
MORTON, Nicola
MOSELEY, Sheila
MOSS, Claudine
MOSS, Jasmin
MOSSACK, Jennifer
MOSSACK, Karin
MOSSBERG, Erik

MOSIMAN, Philipp
MUGLISTON, Victoria
MULLINS, Derith
MURIE, Rosamond
MURRAY, Ingrid
MURRAY, Julia
MURRAY, Regen
MURRAY, Sedonia
MUSKER, Juliet

NABORS, Lisa
NAESS, Katinka
NAFA, Ramsay
NAIDOO, Luc
NANDA, Husna Tara
NANDA, Noor Priya
NANGLE, Patrick
NANGLE, Simone
NASCIMENTO, Andrea
NASH, Tyrella
NASIR, Khalid
NASIR, Rana
NASIR, Rula
NASSER, Dania
NASSER-ZIA, Homaira
NASSIR, Hana
NATHOO, Shirin
NAVARRO, Caroline
NEAVE, Jennifer
NEAVE, Simon
NEELE, Bernardo
NEERMAN, Amanda
NELSON, Timothy
NEWBON, Elizabeth
NEWMAN, Siu Lan
NEWMAN, Susan
NEWTON, Clare
NEWTON, James
NIOTIS, Bessy
NISHINO, Fuyoko
NISHINO, Izumi
NOAKES, Louise
NOAKES, Sarah
NOALL, Catherine
NOALL, Virginia
NOBLE, Helen
NOEL, Louise

NOLAN, Luke
NOON, Safia
NOORANI, Sebeeha
NOORDUYN, Sasha
NORMAN, Mavis
NOVELLO-HUNT,
    Nicola
NOWILATI, Lana
NOYES, Nicholas
NUTTER, Kane
NUTTER, Kim

OAKE, Elizabeth
OBAIDLY, Scherezhrade
OBAIDLY, Soroya
OBOLENSKY, Alexandra
O'CONNOR, Amy
OGDEN, Karen
OGDEN, Rebecca
OGERMAN, Nicole
OGUNSANYA, Tomleke
O'HARA, Moira
OLIVE, Isabel
OLSEN, Lisa
OLSEN, Monica
OLYMPIOS, John
OPPENHEIMER, Sharon
ORMEROD, Susannah
OROZCO, José
OROZCO, Mercedes
OROZCO, Pilar
ORR, Gail
ORR, Mark
ORR, Patrick
ORR, Virginia
ORTIZ-GALAN, Norma
O'SHEA, Sita
OSNOS, Kathryn
OTLEY WARD-
    JACKSON, Elizabeth
OWEN-BOX, Raquel
OWENS, Catherine
OWENS, Timothy

PACK, Melissa
PAGE, Kendall
PALLIDINO, Sabrina

PALMER BECRET,
    Charlotte
PALOS, Brett
PALOS, Stasha
PANIGUIN, Helen
PAPADOPOULOS, Lisa
PAPADOPOULOS,
    Michelle
PAPALIOS, Suzy
PARDELLOUS, Louisa
PARK, Jean
PARKER, Julie
PARKER, Simon
PARMITER, Anne
PARMITER, Anthony
PARRINO, Daniella
PARSONS, Emma
PARTINI, Diana
PARTINI, Tom
PASSEY, Claire
PATTERSON, Elizabeth
PAUL, Abbe
PAUL-REYNAUD,
    Charlotte
PAUL-REYNAUD,
    Francois
PAVLOPOULOS, Eleni
PAVLOPOULOS, Marie
PEARCE, Anne
PEARCE, Carolina
PEARCE, James
PEARCE, Vicki
PEARSON, Candida
PEARSON, Tamar
PEERA, Aseef
PELL, Leslie
PENNEY, Bridget
PENNEY, Caroline
PENNEY, David
PENROSE, Rebecca
PEPPIATT, Catherine
PEREIRA, Francesca
PEREIRA, Natasha
PEREIRA, Victoria
PERONACE, Asa
PERONACE, Davide
PERONACE, Michaela

PETERS, Dylan
PETERS, Fuschia
PETERS, Heidi
PETERS, Tracy
PHIBBS, Harry
PHIBBS, Jessica
PHIBBS, Rebekah
PHILIBERT, Marjorie
PHILLIMORE, Annabella
PHILLIMORE, Francis
PHILLIMORE, Miranda
PHILLIP, Joanne
PHILLIP, Lisa
PHILLIPS, Georgiana
PIERCE, Jill
PINAUD, Paule Emanuelle
PINCKNEY, Emily
PINKO, Christopher
PINKO, Nicole
PINTO, Flavia
PINTO, Lisa
PIZANI, Desireé
PIZZARDA, Alessandra
PLATOU, Jeanette
PLAYFAIR, Miranda
PLUMMER, Katy
PLUMMER, Rachel
POCOCK, Griselda
POCOCK, Michael
PONS, Joanna
POOLE, Angelica
POPAT, Shairose
POPE, Pamela
PORRETT, Susan
PORTER, Allison
PORTERFIELD, Tessa
POST, Clarissa
POTAMINOS, Fokion
POUR, James
POUR, Katie
POWELL, Columba
POWER, Anna
PRESINGER, Ann
PRIESTLY, Max
PRINGLE, Emily
PRIOR, Sarah Jane
PRISLEY, Michael

PRITCHARD, Guy
PROUDLOVE, Lucy
PRUD'HOMME, Emily
PRUD'HOMME, Julia
PUCHNER, Eric
PUCHNER, Laurel
PUCHNER, Penny
PUCHNER, Roderic
PUIG DE LA BELLACASA,
    Maria-Carla
PUNCELES, Antoinette
PUNCUH, Tanya

RACKE, Duco
RACKE, Quinno
RADOMIR, Michael
RAHIMI, Reza
RAHIMI, Yasmin
RAIS, Mahmoud
RAMSAY, Aramynta
RAMSAY, Bonella
RAMSAY, Sholto
RANA, Ambica
RANA, Bhavani
RAOUF, Dina
RAOUF, Sherine
RAWSON, Caroline
RAWSON, Gina
READER, Heidi
READER, Sheila
REDMAN, Christopher
REDMAN, Nicola
REED, Anna Christina
REED, Joanna
REED, Jonathan
REED, Leanda
REICHARDT, Manuela
REID, Frances
REID, Pamela
REID, Sonia
REIFFEN, Catherine
REIS, Samantha
REISSMANN, Angela
REMICK, Charlotte
REMICK, Elizabeth
REMONDET, Barbara
REMØY, Iselin

REMØY, Rebecca
REMØY, Sebastian
REMØY, Susanna
RENWICK, Robin
RENWICK, Suzie
REYNOLDS, Carolyn
RHOODIE, Cosette
RHOODIE, Egon
RICHARDS, Charl
RICHARDS, Samantha
RICHMOND-WATSON,
    Alice
RIGAMONTI, Flandina
RIGG-MILNER, Victoria
RILE, Kathy
RITZ, Margit
ROBB, Camilla
ROBB, Sarah
ROBERTS, Amanda
ROBERTS, Claudia
ROBERTS, Hunter
ROBERTS, Jane
ROBERTS, Susannah
ROBERTSON, Brian
ROBERTSON, Mark
ROBINSON, Alicia
ROBINSON, Caroline
RODDEY, Suci
RODRIGUE, Carolyn
ROE, Edith
ROE, Evelyn
ROE, Michael
ROGERS, Annabel
ROLLO, William
ROMANI, Francesca
ROMARTIER,
    Christopher
ROSENWALD, Celia
ROSENWALD, Gina
ROSIGNOLI, Alan
ROSIGNOLI, Sandra
ROSLAND, Suzanne
ROSMAN, Pat
ROSMAN, Vivien
ROSS, Catherine
ROSS, Celine
ROSS, Suzanne

ROSSETTI, Maria Carla
ROSSETTI, Rosa
ROUNDY, Cathy
ROWE, Antonia
ROWNTREE, Louise
ROYAL, Katrina
ROYDEN, Emma
RUBIN, Patsy
RUGGE-PRICE, Juliet
RUGGE-PRICE, Lucy
RUIZ, Gabriela
RUIZ, Walid
RUSSELL, Alisa
RUSSELL, Edward
RUSSELL, Josephine
RUSSELL, Monika
RUSSELL, Victoria
RUTHERFORD, Camilla
RUTHERFORD, Laetitia
RYYKEN, Jessica

SABBAGH, Deena
SABBAGH, Dyala
SACHAK, Rukaya
SACKS, Angela
SADATI, Easad
SADATI, Merhnaz
SADATI, Seyed
SADRI, Savenaz
SAFFARI, Shohreh
SAHAKAIN, Haik
SAHAKAIN, Marlyne
SAINSBURY, Sarah
SALES, Alexandra
SALES, Christian
SALIH, Eren
SALIH, Erson
SALIH, Esen
SALINGER, Gregory
SAMIY, Maryam
SAMUEL, Jonalla
SAMUEL, Lowina
SAMUELSON, Victoria
SANGER, Daniella
SANTOS, Victoria
SARGENT, Susan
SATTARIPOUR, Ladan

SATTARIPOUR, Rana
SAUNDERS, Elizabeth
SAUNDERS, Emma
SAUNDERS, Justin
SAUNDERS, Tabitha
SAUNDERS, Will
SAUTER, Serena
SAVAGE, Lesley
SAVVA, Marianne
SCARLOTOS, Vincent
SCHENDLER, Bunny
SCHENKER, Juliet
SCHOMAKER, Kim
SCHULZE, Elizabeth
SCHULZE, Kathryn
SCHWARB, Daniella
SCHWEITZER, Grace Ann
SCOTT, Manuela
SCOTT, Virginia
SCOTT-RUSSELL, Holly
SCOTT-RUSSELL, Rory
SEAGAR, Ashleigh
SEARIGHT, Anne
SEARIGHT, Sarah
SEARLE, Kendall
SEARLE, Renée
SEARLE, Rowan
SEBASTIAN, Annie Laurie
SEBASTIAN, David
SEDGWICK, Adam
SEGRAVE, Caroline
SEGRAVE, Rohese
SELZER, Daniel
SELZER, Laura
SENIOR, Trini
SENTONGO, Lena
SENTONGO, Sam
SEPEHRI, Ali
SEPEHRI, Hamid
SERAGELDIN, Karima
SERAGELDIN, Zina
SETTE, Barbara
SETTY, Nicole
SEVAUX, Julien
SEWELL, Emma
SEYMOUR, Daisy

SEYMOUR-NEWTON,
  Rupert
SHAFTEL, Alexandra
SHAHANDEH, Shahpari
SHAKER, Sherine
SHAMSHER, Babbie
SHAMSI, Jenine
SHAMSI, Samina
SHARGHI, Neda
SHARIFF, Maha
SHARP, Jeremy
SHARP, Susannah
SHAW, Danielle
SHAW, Patrick
SHEENAN, Charles
SHEHAB, Sarah
SHEPARD, Christopher
SHEPARD, Lorenzo
SHEPHERD, Joanna
SHERMAN, Alexandra
SHERREN, Fiona
SHERREN, Katie
SHILLING, Kim
SHILLING, Lisa
SIEKMAN, Betsy
SIMO, Eric
SIMO, Janette
SIMO, Rebecca
SIMMONDS, Nicholas
SIMMONDS, William
SIMPSON, Anna
SIMPSON, Paula
SIMS, Camilla
SINCLAIR, Debra
SINCLAIR, Jay
SINCLAIR, Joseph
SINCLAIR, Tamsin
SINCLAIR, Zara
SINGER, Hilary
SINGTON, Louisa
SKEMP, Alison
SKEMP, Brigid
SKEMP, Patrick
SLACK, Alexander
SLACK, Gavin
SLACK, Marika
SLADE, Priscilla

SLATER, Jeannie
SLATER, Louisa
SLOAN, Katie
SMITH, Michaela
SMITH, Phillipa
SNOW, Julia
SOKER, Omer
SORECK, Jennifer
SOSKIN, Amanda
SOSLAND, Meyer
SOTO, Carolina
SPARKS, Carl
SPARKS, Rebecca
SPURDLE, Margaret
SPURDLE, Sarah
STADDON, Stephanie
STADDON, Vanessa
STAFFORD
    NORTHCOTE, Ashley
STANLEY, Alida
STANLEY, Petra
STANLEY, Serge
STANSBY, Daniella
STAUNTON, Jocelyn
STAUNTON, Melissa
STEEL, Caroline
STEEL, Nicola
STEEL, Richard
STEELE, Susannah
STEINBERG, Scott
STEINER, Sarah
STEPHENSON, Clare
STEWART, Amanda
STEWART, Clare
STEWART, Hilary
STEWIN, Anna
STOBY, Lara
STOCK, Elwyn
STOCKTON, Adela
STOCKTON, Henrietta
STONEHAM, Phyllis
STRANGHOENER,
    Carey
STRANKS, Susan
STRATTON, Victoria
STRONG, Margaret
STRONG, Mary Lou

STRONG, Martha
STULTS, Virginia
SUCCI, Anna
SUISSA, Justine
SUISSA, Michael
SUISSA, Samantha
SUTTON, Bonnie
SUZUKI, Eri
SUZUKI, Mari
SWAN, Lucy
SWENNEY, James
SWEID, Nour
SWIRE, Philip
SWIRE, Sophie
SWOPE, Andrea
SWOPE, Lindsay
SYNOTT, Amanda
SYNOTT, James

TAHER, Sara
TAIT, Gavin
TALDVERA, Patricia
TALEY, Lee
TALEY, Scott
TAMIR, Talia
TANNER, Angela
TAPLEY, Deborah
TATE, John
TATE, Lucy
TAVOULAREOUS,
    Marjorie
TAYLOR, Karen
TAYLOR, Linnet
TAYLOR, Sasha
TEAGUE, Vanessa
TEE, Belinda
TEE, Danielle
TEITLER, Nathalie
TEITLER, Nuria
TELLERMAN, Sarah
TENNANT, Caroline
TENNANT, James
TENNANT, Laura
TENNANT, Lucy
TERQUEM, Igor
TERRY, Tammy
TESSARI, Elizabeth

THEDIM, Maria
THIRLBY, Samantha
THOBAMI, Habiba
THOMAS, Charlotte
THOMAS, Guy
THOMAS, Sheran
THOMAS-FERRAND,
    Sally
THOMPSON, Katherine
THOMSON, Amanda
THOMSON, Penelope
THORNE, Claire
THORNTON, Emily
TIFFIN, George
TILLOTSON, Dale
TISCORNIA, Matilda
TODHUNTER, Alice
TODHUNTER, Samantha
TORCHIA, Andrew
TOUSSAINT, David
TOUSSAINT, Kathryn
TOUSSAINT, Michelle
TRAYERS, Amanda
TREAT, Kathy
TREHEARNE, Jane
TREHEARNE, Lucinda
TREHEARNE MORGAN,
    Jill
TREMEAU, Cecile
TRENCH, Amanda
TRENCH, Jonathan
TRENCH, Kerry
TRENCH, Patsy
TRENCH, Tony
TRESSEDER GRIFFIN,
    James
TRESSEDER GRIFFIN,
    Katherine
TRESISE, Angela
TRESISE, Nicole
TRICOGLOU, Eleni
TROUBRIDGE, Tom
TRYON, Charles
TRYON, Zoe
TURLEY, Nigel
TURNER, Catherine
TURNER, Christopher

TURNER, Rebecca
TWINBERROW, Deborah

ULMAN, Morrison
URE, Tessa

VACI, Sarah
VAKIL, Sharenne
VALASCO, Paula
VALENTINE, Sibella
VANDERWAL, Katherine
VANDERWAL, Lisa
VANDERWAL, Peter
VAN GERBIG, Camilla
VAN GERBIG, Eliza
VAUGHAN, Alexis
VAUGHAN, Sasha
VICK, Amanda
VIEHMAN, Sydney
VILJOEN, Clarissa
VILLIERS, Charlotte
VINTON, Chandler
VIRANI, Alka
VIRANI, Mylam
VIVIAN, Charles
Von ARENTSCHILDT,
    Anne
Von BERG, Katherina
Von HOLKE, Constantine
Von SCHMIDT PAULI,
    Katherine
Von STEIN, Daniel
Von STEIN, Sebastien
Von WALDOW, Donata
Von WALDOW, Titina

WADHAM, Lucy
WAINES, Reem
WALKER, Kate
WALKER, Louise
WALLBANK, Judith
WALLER-STEINER,
    Ingrid
WARD-JACKSON,
    Alexander
WARD-JACKSON,
    Charles

WARE, Anne
WARMINGTON, Lara
WARNER, Orlando
WARREN, Catriona
WATKINS, Ingrid
WATSON, Rosemary
WATSON-WALKER, Ann
WAX, Alexandra
WAX, Jonathan
WEBB, Olga
WEIL, Maya
WEIL, Tara
WEIR, Lorna
WEIR, Nicola
WEISSMULLER, Nina
WELCH, Damon
WELCH, Tahnee
WENMAN, Eric
WENMAN, Faye
WEST, Frederica
WEST, Liane
WEST, Lionel
WEST, Lucinda
WEST, Nicola
WEST, Samantha
WESTON, Jana
WHALEY, Catherine
WHITTALL, Sarah
WHYTE, Caroline
WICKREMASINGHE,
    Karla
WIDMAN, Dajana
WILD, Michael
WILDMAN, Tarik
WILLIAMS, Amanda
WILLIAMS, Andrew
WILLIAMSON, George
WILLIAMSON, Nancy
WILSON, David
WILSON, Frederick
WILSON, Jason
WILSON, Jennifer
WILSON, Jessica
WILSON, Kara
WILSON, Keith
WILSON, Louise
WILSON, Norman

WILSON, Raymond
WILSON, Samantha
WISE, Kathryn
WOLFE-DAIMPRE,
    Amanda
WOLLOSHIN, Annabel
WOLMAN, Jacqueline
WOLMAN, Nicole
WOLMAN, Steven
WOOD, Francesca
WOOD, Theodore
WOODFIELD, Susan
WOODLAND, Fleur
WOODLEY, Louise
WOODWARD, Phillipa
WOOLLAM, Edmund
WOLPE, Deborah
WOLPE, Paul
WOLPE, Sarah
WOLPE, Toby
WORMALD, Ana Maria
WORMALD, Valerie
WRIGHT, Kim
WULFSON, Jason
WUNDRAM, Carey
WUNDRAM, Christopher
WUNDRAM, Erin
WYNDHAM-FOUND,
    Bobbie
WYNDHAM-FOUND,
    Tessa
WYNESS, Jeannie
WYNN-POPE, Rosamond

YOUNG, Miranda
YOUNGMAN, Sandra

ZABIH, Leyla
ZAKI, Mohammed
ZAMBARAKGI, Achmed
ZAMBARAKGI, Tarek
ZANGRILLI, Fabrizio
ZAPHIRIOU, Alexandra
ZAPHIRIOU, Paul
ZOLFAGHRI, Fariba
ZOLFAGHRI, Nazila
ZUCCO, Christine

Roll of Former Staff
1928–1987, London and Surrey

Again, we have to apologise for the omission of some surnames of valued teachers due to the loss of essential records. The full names of the Misses Alice, Claire, Laura, Sara, Sheila, Susan and Winnie will (hopefully) be revealed to us in time for a second edition of this history.

MISS PIPPA Akhurst
MISS PAULINE (Mrs Anderson)
MISS MARY (Mrs Arthur)
MISS IRENE Ashton
MISS DEBORAH Binnington
MISS FIONA Boardman
MRS Doreen BOULTON
MISS JENNY Brown
MISS ANNE Butterfield
MISS PATRICIA Cadogan
MISS ALICE Chambers
MISS MARIE Condron-Bain
MISS JANICE (Mrs Crabbe)
MISS MARJORIE Crawford
MADAME Michelle DORKEL
MISS ZARA Duncan
MISS JANICE Foley
MISS NICOLA Gaines
MISS DOREEN Gardiner
MISS ELAINE Goodchild
MRS Dawn GOODSON
MADAME Janine GRAVES (Graves-Gapp)
MISS JANE Greenish

MISS SUSAN Gutteridge
MISS SERENA Hartley
MR RICHARD Heyes
MISS AMANDA Howard
MISS DIANE Husbands
MRS Marie INCE
MRS Dorothy IND
MISS ELOISE Jacobs
MISS JANE Jameson
MADAME Odette JARDIN
MISS VERONICA (Mrs Kalakehe)
MR David KEMP
MISS FAWZIA Khan
MISS CHRIS Kirkness
MISS SHIRLEY Knowles
MADEMOISELLE PASCALE Lavarello
MISS GILL Leach
MISS HILARY Lightfoot
THE LADY LISLE
MISS MARY Lloyd
MISS ANTHEA Maccoy
MISS LUCINDA Mackworth-Young
LADY McCOWAN

MRS Mavis McCREE
MRS Maureen McWATT
MISS ANN Manningham–Buller
MISS JO (Mrs Martin)
MISS AUDREY Meadows
MISS MASSEY (Mrs Modjahedi)
MISS PATRICIA Morris
MISS ROZ (Mrs Mueller)
MISS KATHLEEN Munn
MISS JACKIE Novak
MISS HELEN (Mrs Oberg-Brown)
MISS Pauline PALMER
MISS BARBARA Paulo
MISS ANNE Parmiter
MISS CHRISTINE Parker
MISS FREDA Green (Mrs Pavey)
MRS Betty PECK
MRS Ludmilla POWER
MISS CAROLYN Pride
MISS CAROLYN (Mrs Pringle)
MISS PAT (Mrs Prier)
MISS MARY Powrie

MISS Peggy RENTON
MADAME Jacline REVELL-SMITH
MISS PHILIPPA Roberts
MISS FENELLA (Mrs Rosenwald)
MISS KAY Seth-Smith
MISS ANN (Mrs Sharp)
MISS JULIA Smellie
MRS Elizabeth SMITH
MISS PATRICIA (Mrs Stacey)
MISS DEIDRE Stirling
MISS ELAINE Stoddart
MISS PERRY (Mrs Swingler)
MRS Margaret TURNPENNY
MR Bertie USBORNE
MISS PATRICIA (Mrs Von Simson)
MR Nicholas WEBB
MISS RACHEL Weller
MISS WENDY Wickwire
DR Hilde WOLPE
MRS Margaret WOLPE
MRS Judith WOOD

No school or group of schools can operate efficiently without the skilled services of administrative and other specialist personnel. The Hampshire Schools have been fortunate to be assisted by:

Mr PETER Bailey
Miss ROSANNA Bickerton
Mr Peter BYRNE
Mr Alan FABES
Mr John FURLONG
Mrs Margaret HUNT
Miss Kathleen KEEP
Madame ANGELA Laflaquière
Madame COLETTE Mazet
Mr John McDOUGALL
Miss Elisabeth MOREL

Mrs Lily MUNDEN
Mrs LILY Nunan
Mrs LYN Ouali
Monsieur GEORGES Pestourie
Mrs Margaret PLUMMER
Mr Ron RAWSTRON
Mrs Susannah SIMS
Mrs Sheila TAPLEY
Mr GORDON Taylor
Mrs Shirley WOOLFSON
Mrs Lily WOOTTON

Index

PROGRAMME

	Susan Stranks
	The Pupils
	The Small Girls and Boys
	Anna Goodman and Simon de Wardener
	Patricia Beckwith, Lois Cowin and Wendy Cooper
	Victoria Clinkard, Sandra Donat, Julia Higgs, Melanie Mackenzie, Virginia Orr and Sarah Wolpe
	Susan Stranks
DS	Patricia Beckwith, Gylda Bunday, Wendy Cooper, Carole Dowell, Lois Cowin, Penny Goodwin, Susan Hampshire, Gail Horsfall and Gillian McIver

Lucinda Adler, Georgina Barker, Sandra Chapman, Gillian and Fiona Crampton-Smith, Andrew Donaldson, Sherry D'Oyly, Ann Fox, Anthony and Veronica Elliott, Anthony Fuller, Marie Gale, Eve Grainger, Nicholas Jack, Joanna and Andrew James, Cynthia Johnson, Rivers and Charlotte Job, Penelope Masser, Rafat and Rifat Mahmood, Robin Milne, Jennifer Neave, Diana Newson, Anna Christina Reed, Suzannah Roberts, Pat and Vivian Rosman, Alison and Brigid and Patrick Skemp, Phillipa Smith, Joanna and Sarah Shellard, Jeanette Stevenson, Silas Suchanek, Heather Wilson, Phillipa Woodward, Jacqueline Wolman, Deborah Wolpe, Sandra Youngman, Elizabeth Thornley and Dale Tillotson.

idea of the Gopak !
David Collis, Richard and Andrew Donaldson, Anthony Elliott, Anthony Fuller, John and Nicholas Jack, Rivers Job, Andrew James, Anthony Kelson, Tom Ia Dell, Robin Milne, Charl Richards, Patrick Skemp and Silas Suchanek.

	The Girls
	The Pupils
ERVAL	

1. America Bound !

WATERLOO STATION . . . . Senior Pupils leaving for the U.S.A.

S.S. ILE DI FRANCE. SUR LE PONT PROMENADE.

A 7 HEURES · · · David Collis, Anthony Elliott, Anthony Fuller, Anthony Kelson, Tom La Dell, Charl Richards, Patricia Beckwith, Gylda Bunday, Wendy Cooper, Lois Cowin, Carole Dowell, Susan Hampshire, Gail Horsfall, Gillian McIver and Susan Stranks

LE CHAT BLANC . . . . Deborah Wolpe

A 16 HEURES. AU SALON — Rosemary Allen, Christina Barton, Marchetta Bocca, Iris Campbell, Carol D'Oyly, Georgina Barker, Victoria Burgess, Andrew and Frances Donaldson, Victoria Clinkard, Gillian and Fiona Crampton-Smith, Sandra Donat, Veronica Elliott, Marie Gale, Anna Goodman, Anna Finch, Julia Higgs, Catherine Hopewell-Ash, Joanna and Andrew James, Cynthia Johnson, Rivers Job, Nicholas Jack, Penelope and Sally Masser, Susan Mazet, Rifat and Rahat Mahmood, Robin Milne, Jennifer Neave, Diana Newson, Gail and Virginia Orr, Jill Pierce, Helen Panigson, Anna Christina Reed, Suzannah Roberts, Pat and Vivian Rosman, Aimon and Brigid and Patrick Skemp, Silas Suchanek, Sarah and Joanna Shellard, Heather Wilson, Deborah and Sarah Wolpe.

A 22 HEURES. SOIRÉE DE GALA — Members of St Saviour's, Westminster, Youth Club :—
Betty and Margaret Britland, Pat Collinson, Rosemarie Dukes, David Gable, David Graham, David and Stella Jenkins, Coral May, Jocelyn Newbury and Ray Passenger.

A 22 HEURES. LES PRÉPARATIONS POUR LE CABARET.
LES DANSEUSES — Patricia Beckwith, Gylda Bunday, Wendy Cooper, Carole Dowell, Lois Cowin, Gail Horsfall, Susan Hampshire and Susan Stranks

LA FEMME DE CHAMBRE · · · · · · Susan Hampshire

LE MOUSSE · · · · · · · · Simon de Wardener

LES PETITES FILLES — Veronica Elliott, Anna Finch, Penelope Masser, Alison Skemp

MONSIEUR CHRISTOPHE GRAINGER VOUS PRÉSENTERA

LES BELLES PARISIENNES

SOPRANO · · · · · · · · Susan Hampshire

POLKA · · · · · · · · Gail Horsfall

UNE JEUNE FILLE · · · · · · · Carole Dowell

LES MATELOTS

L'ARRIVÉE. NEW YORK · · · Senior Pupils arrive in the U.S.A. Welcome to America !